You are my
Grammar &
Speaking

2
Workbook

Iam books

You are my
Grammar &
Speaking ② Workbook

Published by

I am Books

#1116, Daeryung Techno Town 12ᵗʰ Bldg.,

14, Gasan digital 2-ro, Geumcheon-gu, Seoul 153-778, Republic of Korea

TEL: 82-2-6343-0999

FAX: 82-2-6343-0995

Visit our website: http://www.iambooks.co.kr

Publishers: Shin Sunghyun, Oh Sangwook
Author: Lucifer EX
Editor: Kim Hyeona

ISBN: 978-89-6398-094-2 63740

Contents

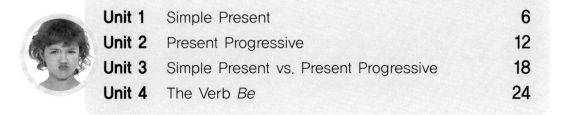
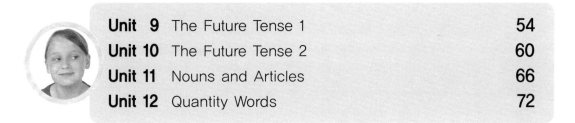

After Finishing the Workbook

Book 2

Teacher's Comments

Parents' Comments

Class

Name

Unit **1** Simple Present

Unit Focus
- ▶ Affirmatives and Negatives
- ▶ Spelling Rules
- ▶ *Yes/No Questions*
- ▶ Simple Present as a Future Tense

Learn & Practice

Simple Present: Affirmatives, Negatives

- 현재 시제는 현재의 일상적인 습관이나 반복되는 동작 또는 일반적인 사실이나 불변의 진리를 나타내요.
- 일반 동사의 부정은 동사 바로 앞에 do not 또는 does not을 붙여요. 주어가 3인칭 단수인 경우에만 does not을 써요.
  일상 영어에서는 don't, doesn't를 씁니다. 이때의 do, does는 조동사(helping verb)예요.

True	Fact	Daily Routine
Plants **need** water and sunlight.	Bears **sleep** in the winter.	Every day she **runs** along the beach.

Affirmative

| I
You
We
They | **run.** | He
She
It
Tom | **runs.** |

Negative

| I
You
We
They | **don't run.** | He
She
It
Mary | **doesn't run.** |

Ⓐ **Rewrite each sentence with the new subject in parentheses.**

1. I wake up early in the morning. (Kevin) → *Kevin wakes up early in the morning.*

2. We go to work at 8:00. (Jane) → _____

3. He loves his country. (they) → _____

4. I take the children to the beach. (Wilson) → _____

Ⓑ **Complete the sentences with the negative form of the verbs in brackets.**

1. Tom ___*doesn't go*___ to school on the weekend. (go)

2. Abby _____ with her sister's homework. (help)

3. Nonliving things _____ water and sunlight. (need)

4. On Wednesday the classes _____ at 9:00. (start)

Simple Present: Spelling Rules of Final -s and -es

- 주어가 3인칭 단수(he, she, Mary, a dog, it...)일 때에만 현재 동사 뒤에 -s나 -es를 붙여 주어가 3인칭 단수임을 알리
  자는 약속이 되어 있어요.

Karen **wears** a school uniform.

He **studies** Korean hard.

She **has** a toothache.

대부분의 동사에 -s를 붙임.	rains - rain**s** speak - speak**s** visit - visit**s** love - love**s**
-o, -s(s), -ch, -sh, -x로 끝나는 동사 뒤에 -es를 붙임.	go - go**es** watch - watch**es** fix - fix**es** do - do**es** wash - wash**es** pass - pass**es** finish - finish**es**
『자음+y』로 끝나는 동사 → -y를 -i로 고치고 -es를 붙임.	try - tr**ies** study - stud**ies** cry - cr**ies** fly - fl**ies** copy - cop**ies**
『모음+y』로 끝나는 동사 → 그냥 -s만 붙임.	play - play**s** buy - buy**s** enjoy - enjoy**s** say - say**s** stay - stay**s**
불규칙 변화 동사	have - **has**

A Write the third person singular of the following verbs.

1. sleep → *sleeps*

2. watch → _____

3. copy → _____

4. finish → _____

5. stay → _____

6. enjoy → _____

7. wash → _____

8. have → _____

9. say → _____

B Circle the correct words.

1. (We / My friend) wear old clothes.

2. (You / He) wears a school uniform.

3. (My dad / I) washes the car every Sunday.

4. (He / I) want a new job.

5. (Bread / Books) costs a lot.

6. (You / She) drives too fast.

7. (That child / Children) makes a lot of noise.

8. (That bus / All those buses) go to the station.

Simple Present: *Yes/No* questions

- 일반 동사의 yes/no 의문문은 문장 앞에 do/does를 써요. 주어가 3인칭 단수인 경우에만 does를 쓰고 반드시 동사는 -s, -es를 붙이지 않고 동사 원형을 그대로 써야 해요.
- 대답은 주어에 맞는 do나 does를 이용해서 대답해요.

Q: **Does** Natalie **eat** breakfast every day?
A: **Yes**, she **does**.

Q: **Do** you **have** a car?
A: **No**, I **don't**. I have a bicycle.

A Make *yes/no* questions and complete the short answers.

1. She plays the guitar well.   Q: _Does she play the guitar well?_   A: Yes, _she does_ .

2. He has a pet.   Q: _____   A: No, _____ .

3. They speak Chinese.   Q: _____   A: Yes, _____ .

4. The sun gives us energy.   Q: _____   A: Yes, _____ .

Learn & Practice 4

Simple Present as a Future Tense

- 기차, 비행기, 영화, 공연 시간표와 같이 확실히 정해진 일정에는 현재 시제를 써서 미래를 나타내요.

Q: What time **does** the movie **begin** tomorrow?
A: It **begins** at 10:00 tomorrow morning.

My plane **arrives** at 7:00 tomorrow evening.

A Circle the correct words and check the correct meanings.

1. The concert ((begins)/ begin) at eight tonight.   Future: ___√___   True: _____

2. The bus (leaves / left) at 9:00 tomorrow morning.   Future: _____   Fact: _____

3. Ann (took / takes) a shower every day.   Future: _____   Habit: _____

A Look at the pictures and use the prompts to write sentences.

1.

tomorrow morning / the movie / at 10:00 / start

→ The movie starts at 10:00 tomorrow morning.

2.

tomorrow morning / at 11:00 / arrive / Tom's plane

→ _____

3.

at 8:00 p.m. tomorrow / begin / the soccer game

→ _____

4.

what time / tomorrow / the baseball game / begin / ?

→ _____

B Write what these people *do* or *don't do*.

	study hard	ride a bicycle	swim very well	listen to K-pop music
Peter	✓	✗	✓	✗
Isabella	✗	✓	✗	✓
Tina & Ben	✓	✓	✗	✗
I(about you)				

Peter _studies hard and swims very well, but he doesn't ride a bicycle or listen to K-pop music_.

Isabella _____.

Tina and Ben _____.

I _____.

C Look at the pictures and prompts. Write questions and answers as in the example.

1.

how often / Tom / take out the trash / ?
(once a week)

Q: How often does Tom take out the trash?
A: He takes out the trash once a week.

2.

what / Scott / do / on Saturday mornings / ?
(wash his car)

Q: _____
A: _____

3.

how often / you / study Korean / ?
(four times a week)

Q: _____
A: _____

4.

where / Jessica / go / every day / ?
(go to school)

Q: _____
A: _____

D Write questions and negations as in the example.

1. Nancy lives in Seattle.

Q: Does Nancy live in Seattle?
N: Nancy doesn't live in Seattle.

2. She takes the bus to work.

Q: _____
N: _____

3. Mike and Lee read a lot of newspapers.

Q: _____
N: _____

4. They speak on the phone a lot.

Q: _____
N: _____

5. Jennifer has classes every day.

Q: _____
N: _____

A Look at the example and practice with a partner. Use the words below or invent your own. (Repeat 3 times.)

1.

 Let's get sushi!

 No, I hate sushi, but I love pizza. Do you like pizza?

 Yes, I do. Let's get pizza!

1.
sushi
→ No / pizza

2.
hamburger
→ No / French fries

3.
tomatoes
→ No / string beans

4.
vegetables
→ No / chocolate ice cream

5.
broccoli
→ No / sandwiches

B Work with a partner to make conversations. Begin your answers with *no*.

 Olivia / play tennis / on Sundays?
→ No / watch TV

 Susan / take out / the trash / every day?
→ No / twice a week

 Cindy / read a magazine / in the mornings?
→ No / a newspaper

 Wilson / do the dishes / every morning?
→ No / every evening

Does Olivia play tennis on Sundays?

No, she doesn't. She watches TV.

Your turn now.

 the students / have lunch / at a restaurant?
→ No / the cafeteria

 Yeji / learn / English / every day?
→ No / three times a week

Present Progressive

Unit Focus
- ▶ Affirmatives and Negatives
- ▶ Spelling Rules of Verb-*ing*
- ▶ *Yes/No* Questions

Learn & Practice 1

Present Progressive: Affirmatives, Negatives

- 현재 진행 시제는 말하는 순간, 보고 있는 그 순간에 진행 중인 동작이나 행동을 나타내요. be 동사와 연결하여 'be(am, is, are) + v-ing' 형태를 취하고, 우리말로 '~하고 있다, ~하고 있는 중이다'라는 뜻을 가져요.

- 말하고 있는 순간에 진행 중인 동작 외에 최근에 일시적으로 하고 있는 일을 나타낼 때에도 현재진행형을 사용해요.

- 우리말로 '~하고 있지 않다'라는 부정문을 만들 때에는 be 동사 바로 뒤에 not을 붙이기만 하면 돼요.

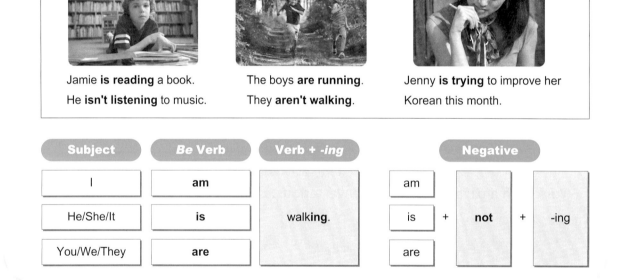

Right Now		Around Now
Jamie **is reading** a book. He **isn't listening** to music.	The boys **are running**. They **aren't walking**.	Jenny **is trying** to improve her Korean this month.

Subject	Be Verb	Verb + -ing		Negative		
I	**am**			am		
He/She/It	**is**	walk**ing**.		is	+ **not** +	-ing
You/We/They	**are**			are		

(A) Fill in the blanks with the present progressive and check.

1. He ___is sitting___ (sit) at the desk.   Right Now: __√__   Around Now: _____

2. She _____ (eat) dinner.   Right Now: _____   Around Now: _____

3. I _____ (study) French this semester.   Right Now: _____   Around Now: _____

4. She _____ (work) hard these days.   Right Now: _____   Around Now: _____

5. We _____ (take) Taekwondo lessons this semester.
          Right Now: _____   Around Now: _____

6. Listen! John _____ (play) the piano.   Right Now: _____   Around Now: _____

Present Progressive: Spelling Rules of Verb-*ing*

go → going　　walk → walking study → studying　　eat → eating	• 대부분의 동사 원형에 -ing를 붙여요.
bake → baking　　take → taking come → coming　　live → living	• -e로 끝나는 동사는 -e를 빼고 -ing를 붙여요.
sit → sitting　　swim → swimming run → running　　cut → cutting	• '단모음＋단자음'으로 끝나는 1음절 동사는 마지막 자음을 한 번 더 쓰고 -ing를 붙여요.

※ 강세가 앞에 있는 동사는 그냥 -ing만 붙여요.

listen → listening　　　open → opening　　　visit → visiting

※ -w, -x, -y로 끝나는 동사는 마지막 자음을 한 번 더 쓰지 않고 그냥 -ing만 붙여요.

show → showing　　　fix → fixing　　　say → saying

A Add -*ing* to the verbs below and put them in the correct column.

play	work	swim	stop	write	read
make	sit	run	come	love	eat

walk → walking	ride → riding	cut → cutting
playing		

B Complete the sentences with the verbs in brackets. Use the present progressive.

1. Tony _____is working_____ in the garden. (work)

2. They _____ to music. (listen)

3. Justin _____ his blog. (make)

4. They _____ hamburgers in a fast food restaurant now. (eat)

Present Progressive: *Yes/No* Questions

- 의문문을 만들 때에는 be 동사의 의문문 만드는 방법과 똑같아요. be 동사를 문장 맨 앞으로 보내고 물음표(?)만 붙이면 돼요. 대답도 yes/no를 이용해 알맞은 be 동사로 대답해요. '~하고 있니?' 또는 '~하고 있는 중이니?'라는 뜻을 가져요.

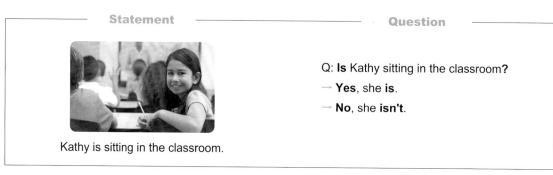

Statement	Question
Kathy is sitting in the classroom.	Q: **Is** Kathy sitting in the classroom**?** → **Yes**, she **is**. → **No**, she **isn't**.

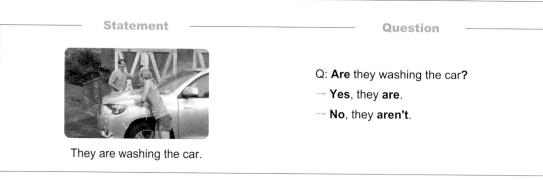

Statement	Question
They are washing the car.	Q: **Are** they washing the car**?** → **Yes**, they **are**. → **No**, they **aren't**.

- 일상 영어에서 no로 대답할 때 주로 축약형을 쓰지만 긍정의 대답에는 축약형을 쓰지 않아요.

Be Verb	Subject	Verb + *-ing*
Am	I	
Is	she/he/it	dancing?
Are	you/we/they	

Ⓐ Make *yes/no* questions in the present progressive. Then complete the short answers.

1. she / buy the striped shirt
Q: *Is she buying the striped shirt?* A: Yes, *she is* .

2. it / rain outside
Q: _____ A: No, _____ .

3. they / shop now
Q: _____ A: Yes, _____ .

4. you / wear your new blouse
Q: _____ A: No, _____ .

5. she / smile at me
Q: _____ A: No, _____ .

6. he / stay in a hotel near the sea
Q: _____ A: Yes, _____ .

A Use the prompts to make sentences about each picture, one affirmative and one negative. Use the present progressive.

1. the baby: cry loudly / sleep
   → The baby is crying loudly.
   → He isn't sleeping.

2. Lucy: watch TV / talk on the phone
   → _____
   → _____

3. Eric: run on a track / play the violin
   → _____
   → _____

4. Ava and Peter: have lunch / see a scary movie
   → _____
   → _____

B Look at the picture. Read the questions and answer them.

Bob and his wife Nancy are playing with their baby Steve in the park.

1. What are Bob and Nancy doing?
   They're playing with their baby Steve.

2. Where are they playing?
   _____

3. What is Steve wearing?
   _____

4. Who is wearing a hood?
   _____

5. Who is holding the baby's arm?
   _____

C Look at the pictures. Use the prompts to ask and answer as in the example.

1.

the boys / play soccer?
→ No / basketball

Q: Are the boys playing soccer?

A: No, they aren't. They are playing basketball.

2.

your sister / work on her computer now?
→ No / have lunch

Q: _____

A: _____

3.

Jessica / read a comic book
→ No / study math

Q: _____

A: _____

4.

Scott / wash the car now?
→ No / do the laundry

Q: _____

A: _____

D All the statements below are incorrect. Look at the picture and write correct negative and affirmative statements. Use the present progressive.

1. The man and the woman are standing in the street.
   → The man and the woman aren't standing in the street. They are sitting in a car.

2. The man is working on a laptop.
   → _____
   _____

3. The woman is speaking on the phone.
   → _____
   _____

4. It is raining.
   → _____
   _____

5. The man is holding a wallet.
   → _____
   _____

A Look at the example and practice with a partner. Use the words below or invent your own. (Repeat 3 times.)

I.

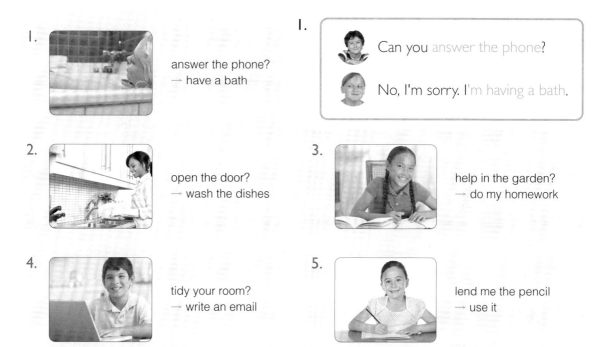

answer the phone?
→ have a bath

I.

Can you answer the phone?

No, I'm sorry. I'm having a bath.

2.

open the door?
→ wash the dishes

3.

help in the garden?
→ do my homework

4.

tidy your room?
→ write an email

5.

lend me the pencil
→ use it

B Work with a partner. Look at the pictures and make two sentences about each person. In the first sentence, describe what is not true. In the second sentence, describe what is true.

Tom isn't wearing a hat.
He's wearing a white shirt.
Your turn now.

The mother isn't...

Alan: wear a hat (X)
→ a white shirt (O)

the mother: stand next to the bride (X)
→ the groom (O)

David: play the violin (X)
→ the saxophone (O)

the man: sit on the sofa (X)
→ the floor (O)

Sarah: work in the garden (X)
→ at her office right now (O)

Amy: read a book (X)
→ a magazine (O)

Simple Present vs. Present Progressiv

▶ Meaning & Uses of Simple Present and Present Progressive
▶ *Always* + Present Progressive
▶ Present Progressive as a Future Tense

Learn & Practice 1

Simple Present and Present Progressive

- 현재 시제는 일상적인 습관 또는 반복되는 동작을 나타낼 때 사용해요. 특히 과학적 사실이나 변하지 않는 진리도 현재 시제를 써서 표현해요.

- 진행 시제는 말하는 순간 또는 보고 있는 그 순간에 진행 중인 동작이나 행동을 나타내요. 말하고 있는 순간에 진행 중인 동작 외에 최근에 일시적으로 하고 있는 일을 나타낼 때에도 현재진행형을 사용해요.

Simple Present	Present Progressive
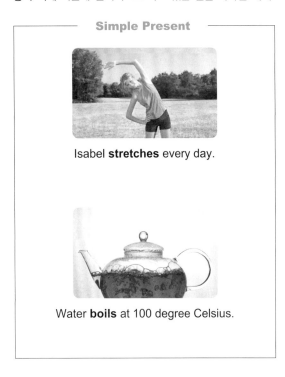	

Isabel **stretches** every day.

Isabel **is stretching** now.

Water **boils** at 100 degree Celsius.

Water **is boiling**. Could you turn it off?

- 현재 시제와 현재진행 시제는 다음과 같은 시간 표현들과 함께 자주 쓰여요.

Simple Present

Time Expressions

every morning/day/week/year, etc.
on Monday/Tuesday, etc.
in the morning/afternoon/evening
always, never, sometimes, often, etc.

I *usually* **read** the newspaper *in the morning*.
We **have** a party on my birthday *every year*.

Present Progressive

(Time) Expressions

now, at the moment, at present
these days, today
this week/month/year
Look!, Listen!

My grandma **is staying** with me *these days*.
They **are having** dinner *now*.

A Put the verbs into the correct form, simple present or present progressive.

1. My brother never ___drinks___ (drink) tea in the morning.

2. Let's go out. It _____ (not / rain) now.

3. Olivia is very good at languages. She _____ (speak) three languages very well.

4. Look at that man! He _____ (steal) something.

5. She _____ (have) dinner with her family every evening.

6. Hurry up! The taxi driver _____ (wait) for us.

Learn & Practice 2

Always + Present Progressive

- 빈도 부사(adverbs of frequency)는 현재 시제와 함께 쓰지만 현재진행 시제와는 함께 쓰지 않아요. 빈도 부사의 위치는 be 동사와 조동사 뒤, 그리고 일반 동사 앞에 위치해요.

- always만 현재진행 시제와 함께 쓸 수 있는데, 이때의 always는 '너무 자주(too often)'라는 의미를 담고 있어요. 불평이나 짜증을 나타내는 표현이에요.

─── Every Time ───	─── A Habitual Negative Action ───
The earth **always** goes around the sun.	Oh, no! I left my cell phone at home again. **I'm always forgetting** something.

Adverbs of Frequency	
always	100%
usually	75%
often	50%
sometimes	25%
rarely/seldom	10%
never	0%

George **always** plays tennis on Saturdays.
You must **often** water this kind of plant.
It **often** rains in the summer in Florida.
She **seldom** goes to the zoo.
He is **never** serious.

A Complete the sentences with the words in brackets. Use always *-ing*.

1. I've lost my key again. I ___am always losing___ (lose, always) things.

2. My sister _____ (play, always) the piano loudly.

3. You _____ (watch, always) TV.

4. Jane is never satisfied. She _____ (complain, always).

Present Progressive as a Future Tense

- 어떤 일을 하기로 이미 정해진 개인의 일정인 경우에 현재진행형이 미래를 나타낼 수 있어요.
- 주로 움직임을 나타내는 come, go, stay, arrive, leave나 교통수단을 나타내는 fly, walk, ride, drive, take 등이 자주 쓰여요.

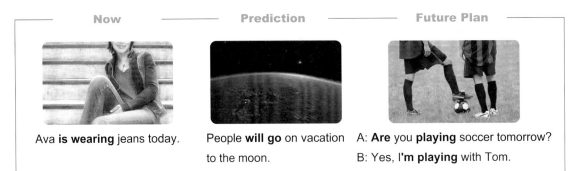

Now	Prediction	Future Plan
Ava **is wearing** jeans today.	People **will go** on vacation to the moon.	A: **Are** you **playing** soccer tomorrow? B: Yes, I**'m playing** with Tom.

- 개인의 정해진 일정이 아닌, 단순히 미래를 예상하거나 추측할 때에는 진행형 시제를 쓰지 않고 'will + 동사 원형'을 써야 해요.

Ⓐ **Read and write** *present* **or** *future.*

1. Where is Nancy? Is she working? → *present*

2. Are you going out tonight? → _____

3. Brian is flying to New York in two hours. → _____

4. I'm seeing Isabel on Wednesday. → _____

5. I am taking three courses this semester. → _____

6. Peter, what are you doing here? → _____

7. We're getting a new car next week. → _____

8. Is Sunny making lunch at the moment? → _____

9. They are going to the theater this evening. → _____

10. I'm going to work tomorrow at 9:00. → _____

A Today is a holiday. Look at the pictures and write what each woman does every day and what they are doing today, as in the example.

1.

(usually / get up)   (today / still / sleep)

→ Olivia _usually gets up at 7:30 every day,_
but today she is still sleeping .

2.

(usually / have breakfast)   (today / watch TV)

→ Jessica _____

_____ .

3.

(usually / drive to work)(today / walk / in the park)

→ Megan _____

_____ .

4.

(usually / learn yoga)   (today / make dinner)

→ Isabel _____

_____ .

B Look at Janet's schedule and complete the sentences as in the example. Use the present progressive.

Monday:	Have lunch with John at 1:00. Go to gym after work.
Tuesday:	attend a meeting from 8:00 to 10:00
Wednesday:	Go to the dentist at 2:00
Thursday:	Give a presentation to her boss at 12:00
Friday:	Go to Peter and Susan's house for dinner at 7:00
Saturday:	Meet Lisa outside the movie theater at 6:00
Sunday:	Play tennis with Nancy at 11:00

1. _She's having lunch with John_ at 1 o'clock on Monday.

2. _____ from 8:00 to 10 o'clock on Tuesday.

3. _____ at 2:00 on Wednesday.

4. _____ at 12:00 on Thursday.

5. _____ at 7:00 on Friday.

6. _____ at 6:00 on Saturday.

7. _____ at 11 o'clock on Sunday.

C Use the pictures and prompts to write questions and answers. Use the simple present or the present progressive as in the example.

1.

What / Jeffrey / usually do / in the evenings / ?

Q: What does Jeffrey usually do in the evenings?

A: He usually stays at home.

stay / at home

2.

What / Tom and Paul / do / this evening / ?

Q: _____

A: _____

play / a board game

3.

What / Sandra / usually eat / for breakfast / ?

Q: _____

A: _____

toast and jam

4.

What / Jennifer / do / now / ?

Q: _____

A: _____

drink / orange juice

D Choose the correct words to complete the sentences. Use *always* and a continuous verb.

| miss | talk | take | bark | laugh | eat |

1. I don't trust my sister. She _____is always taking_____ my clothes without asking me.

2. My friend's dog is so loud. It _____ at the smallest sounds!

3. My math teacher is so funny. We _____ in her class.

4. A: Tom talks too much, doesn't he? B: Yes, and he _____ about soccer.

5. A: Rachel misses lectures much too often in my opinion.

   B: I agree. She _____ lectures.

6. I don't like eating lunch with Sarah. She _____ with her mouth open.

A Look at the example and practice with a partner. Use the words below or invent your own. (Repeat 3 times.)

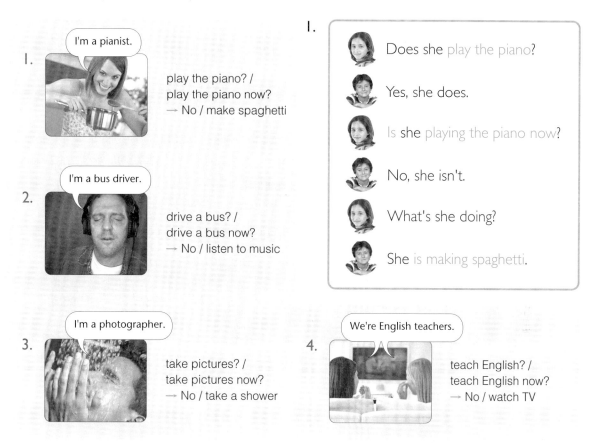

1. I'm a pianist.

play the piano? /
play the piano now?
→ No / make spaghetti

2. I'm a bus driver.

drive a bus? /
drive a bus now?
→ No / listen to music

3. I'm a photographer.

take pictures? /
take pictures now?
→ No / take a shower

4. We're English teachers.

teach English? /
teach English now?
→ No / watch TV

1.

Does she play the piano?

Yes, she does.

Is she playing the piano now?

No, she isn't.

What's she doing?

She is making spaghetti.

B Work with a partner. Ask and answer questions about each person. Use the simple present and the present progressive.

Susan / read a book

Nick / play the saxophone

Amanda / write an email

Jasmine / do her homework

Is Susan reading a book?

Yes, she is.

Does she read a book every day?

Yes, she does.

Your turn to ask now.

Lauren / paint a picture

Kevin / wash the dishes

the children / play soccer

Unit 4 The Verb *Be*

⊛ **Unit Focus**

▶ The Verb *Be*: Affirmatives
▶ The Verb *Be*: Negatives
▶ The Verb *Be*: Yes/No Questions

Present and Past of *Be*: Affirmatives

- be 동사는 주어의 움직임이나 동작을 나타내기보다는 주어의 성질이나 상태를 설명해 주는 말이에요. 현재일 때에는 am, is, are(~이다)를 쓰고, 과거일 때에는 was, were(~이었다)를 써요.

- be 동사 뒤에 부사나 전치사가 있을 때에는 '있(었)다'라는 뜻이 돼요.

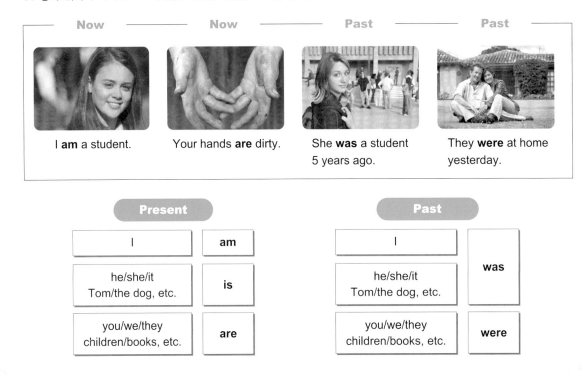

Now	Now	Past	Past
I **am** a student.	Your hands **are** dirty.	She **was** a student 5 years ago.	They **were** at home yesterday.

Present

I	am
he/she/it Tom/the dog, etc.	is
you/we/they children/books, etc.	are

Past

I	was
he/she/it Tom/the dog, etc.	
you/we/they children/books, etc.	were

A Write *am/is/are* (present) or *was/were* (past).

1. I ___was___ busy yesterday. I ___am___ free now.

2. Last year she _____ 20, so she _____ 21 now.

3. Today the weather _____ nice, but yesterday it _____ very cold.

4. A: Where _____ the children? B: I don't know. They _____ here ten minutes ago.

5. His father _____ a doctor 10 years ago. His mother _____ a lawyer now.

Present and Past of *Be*: Negatives

- be 동사의 부정문은 be 동사 바로 뒤에 not만 붙이면 돼요. '~이/가 아니다, 있지 않다'라는 뜻을 가져요.
- be 동사의 과거도 was와 were 바로 뒤에 not만 붙이면 부정문이 돼요. '~이/가 아니었다, 있지 않았다'라는 뜻으로 해석해요.

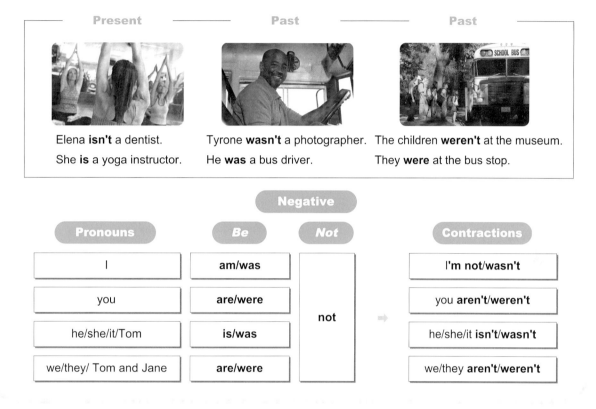

	Present		Past		Past	
	Elena **isn't** a dentist. She **is** a yoga instructor.		Tyrone **wasn't** a photographer. He **was** a bus driver.		The children **weren't** at the museum. They **were** at the bus stop.	

Negative

Pronouns	Be	Not		Contractions
I	am/was			I'm not/wasn't
you	are/were	not	⇒	you aren't/weren't
he/she/it/Tom	is/was			he/she/it isn't/wasn't
we/they/ Tom and Jane	are/were			we/they aren't/weren't

A Make the sentences negative as in the example.

1. She was angry at me. → *She wasn't angry at me.*

2. I'm at home right now. → _____

3. Jane was very tired last night. → _____

4. Our room is very big, and it is very clean. → _____

5. The history books are interesting. → _____

6. Grace and Karen were my classmates. → _____

7. Ten years ago, Jerry was in fifth grade. → _____

Present and Past of *Be*: *Yes/No* Questions

- be 동사의 의문문은 be 동사를 문장 맨 앞으로 보내고 물음표(?)를 써 주면 돼요.
- 대답은 be 동사의 현재형 또는 과거형을 그대로 사용하여 yes나 no로 대답하고, 주어는 알맞은 대명사로 바꾸어 대답하면 됩니다. 부정의 대답은 축약하지만, 긍정의 대답은 축약형을 쓰지 않아요.

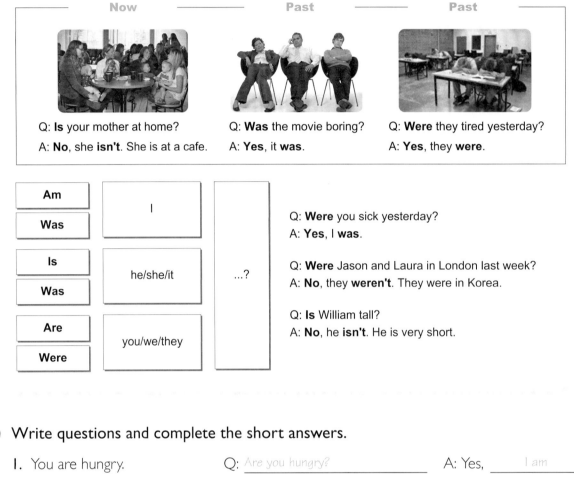

Now	Past	Past
Q: **Is** your mother at home?	Q: **Was** the movie boring?	Q: **Were** they tired yesterday?
A: **No**, she **isn't**. She is at a cafe.	A: **Yes**, it **was**.	A: **Yes**, they **were**.

Am / Was	I	...?
Is / Was	he/she/it	
Are / Were	you/we/they	

Q: **Were** you sick yesterday?
A: **Yes**, I **was**.

Q: **Were** Jason and Laura in London last week?
A: **No**, they **weren't**. They were in Korea.

Q: **Is** William tall?
A: **No**, he **isn't**. He is very short.

Ⓐ Write questions and complete the short answers.

1. You are hungry. Q: *Are you hungry?* _____ A: Yes, ____*I am*____.

2. Mozart was a musician. Q: _____ A: Yes, _____.

3. Thomas Edison was a painter. Q: _____ A: No, _____.

4. Michael Jackson was a singer. Q: _____ A: Yes, _____.

5. He is a basketball team coach. Q: _____ A: No, _____.

6. My parents are young. Q: _____ A: Yes, _____.

A Look at the table. Then write correct answers.

	Country	Job	Age
James	New Zealand	student	12
Hyesu	Korea	actress	20
George	the USA	photographer	32
Sarah	Ireland	dentist	32

1. Q: Is Hyesu a student? A: *No, she isn't. She is an actress.* _____

2. Q: Is Sarah 12 years old? A: _____

3. Q: Is James from New Zealand? A: _____

4. Q: Is George from Korea? A: _____

5. Q: Is Hyesu 27 years old? A: _____

6. Q: Is George a dentist? A: _____

7. Q: Are Sarah and George 20 years old? A: _____

8. Q: Is James an actor? A: _____

B Fill in the blanks with *am*, *is*, *are*, *was*, or *were*.

1.

It ___is___ Monday today. Julie and Nancy ___are___ at work.
It ___was___ Sunday yesterday, and they ___were___ at home.

2.

It _____ midnight now. The children _____ in bed.
They _____ in the living room three hours ago.

3.

It _____ 12 noon, and she _____ in the kitchen.
She _____ in the garden two hours ago.

Ⓒ Look at the pictures. Use the prompts to make questions and answers. Use the past of *be*.

1.

Elvis Presley / a politician?
→ No / a very famous singer

Q: Was Elvis Presley a politician?

A: No, he wasn't. He was a very famous singer.

2.

James Dean / an architect?
→ No / a very famous actor

Q: _____

A: _____

3.

Van Gogh / an engineer?
→ No / a very famous painter

Q: _____

A: _____

4.

Alexander Graham Bell and Thomas Edison / musicians
→ No / very famous inventors

Q: _____

_____

A: _____

_____

Ⓓ Look at the pictures and write questions and answers.

1. Harry / a teacher?

Q: Is Harry a teacher?

A: No, he isn't. He is a police officer.

2. Isabel / a soccer player?

Q: _____

A: _____

3. they / plumbers?

Q: _____

A: _____

4. Susan and Dylan / detectives?

Q: _____

A: _____

A Look at the example and practice with a partner. Use the words below or invent your own. (Repeat 3 times.)

1.
Michael Jackson / an American singer

1.
This is Michael Jackson.

He was an American singer.

2.
Mother Teresa / a Christian Saint

3.
Gustav Klimt / a Austrian painter

4.
Kim Daejung / a President of South Korea

5.
Andre Kim / a fashion designer

B Work with a partner. You choose a job from the pictures and write it on a piece of paper. Your partner asks questions to find out what he/she is.

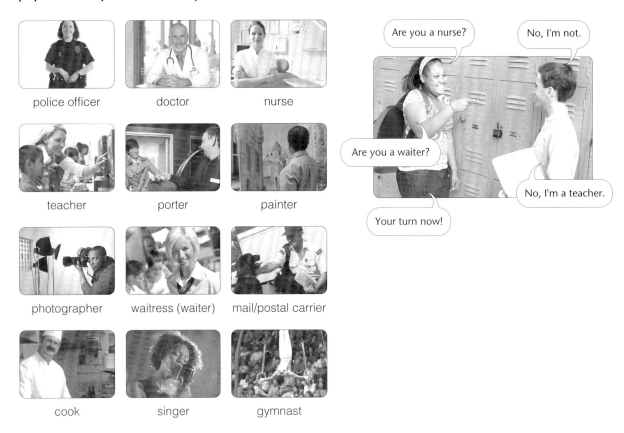

police officer

doctor

nurse

teacher

porter

painter

photographer

waitress (waiter)

mail/postal carrier

cook

singer

gymnast

Are you a nurse?

No, I'm not.

Are you a waiter?

No, I'm a teacher.

Your turn now!

The Verb *Be* **29**

Unit 5 Simple Past 1

Unit Focus

▶ Affirmatives vs. Negatives
▶ Yes/No Questions
▶ Used To: Past Habits

Learn & Practice 1

Simple Past: Affirmatives vs. Negatives

- 과거 시제(simple past)는 이미 끝난 과거의 동작이나 상태를 나타내어 현재와는 아무런 관련이 없어요. 동사에 -(e)d를 붙여서 과거형을 만들고, 주로 yesterday, last night/week/month/year, ago 등과 함께 자주 쓰여요.

- 부정문은 주어의 인칭이나 수와 관계없이 동사 앞에 did not을 쓰고 동사는 원형 그대로 써요. 일상 영어에서는 didn't로 줄여서 써요.

The US Civil War **started** in 1861
and **ended** in 1865.

Jiyun **didn't play** tennis this morning.
She **helped** her mother clean the house.

Affirmative			Negative	
I/We/You He/She/It/They	**walked**.		I/We/You He/She/It/They	**did not** walk. (= **didn't** walk.)

A Circle the correct words and make simple past negative sentences.

1. Harry (work / worked) last Sunday. → *Harry didn't work last Sunday.*

2. I (played / play) hockey yesterday. → _____

3. We (finish / finished) the project last night. → _____

4. They (stayed / stay) at a hotel last week. → _____

5. It (rain / rained) a lot here yesterday. → _____

6. Bill (cooked / cook) the potatoes yesterday. → _____

Simple Past: *Yes/No* Questions

- 의문문은 주어가 무엇이든 관계없이 did를 문장 맨 앞에 쓰고 물음표(?)를 쓰면 돼요. did가 과거임을 나타내기 때문에 주어 뒤에 있는 동사는 반드시 동사 원형을 써야 해요.
- 대답은 yes나 no로 하고, 주어를 알맞은 대명사로 바꿔서 긍정일 때에는 'Yes, + 대명사 주어 + did'로, 부정일 때에는 'No, + 대명사 주어 + didn't.'로 답하면 돼요.

Question

Did your mother **work** as a reporter?

Yes, she **did**.

No, she **didn't**. She worked as a graphic designer.

Did	**Subject**	**Base Verb**	**Answers**	
Did	I/we/you he/she/it/they	dance?	**Yes**, I (we, he...) **did**.	**No**, I (we, he...) **didn't**.

A Make *yes/no* questions and complete the short answers.

1. visit / the Natural History Museum / she / ?
   Q: *Did she visit the Natural History Museum?*   A: No, *she didn't* .

2. travel / by helicopter / he / ?
   Q: _____   A: Yes, _____ .

3. like / tea and cookies / Tom and Jane / ?
   Q: _____   A: No, _____ .

4. watch / the NBC show / the students / ?
   Q: _____   A: Yes, _____ .

5. walk / in Central Park / this morning / Kathy / ?
   Q: _____   A: No, _____ .

6. enjoy / the trip / in Egypt / Brian / ?
   Q: _____   A: Yes, _____ .

Used To: Past Habits

- 'used to + 동사 원형'은 과거에 반복된 행동을 나타내요. 지금은 더 이상 행하지 않는 과거의 동작이므로 현재와는 아무런 관련이 없는 과거 시제랍니다.
- 부정은 'didn't use to'를 쓰고 '예전에는 ~하지 않았는데 지금은 ~하다'라는 뜻을 나타내요.
- 의문문은 'Did + 주어 + use to...?'로 쓰고 yes나 no로 대답해요.

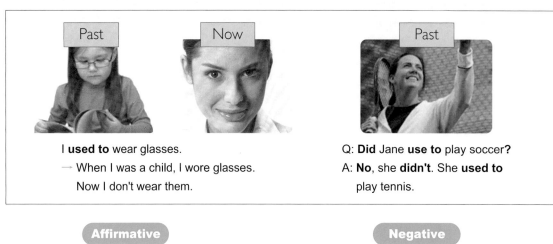

I **used to** wear glasses.
→ When I was a child, I wore glasses. Now I don't wear them.

Q: **Did** Jane **use to** play soccer**?**
A: **No**, she **didn't**. She **used to** play tennis.

Affirmative

| I/We/You He/She/It/They | **used to** | jog. |

Negative

| I/We/You He/She/It/They | **did not** (= didn't) | **use to** jog. |

Question

| **Did** | I/we/you he/she/it/they | **use to** | jog? |

- I **used to** be thin. Now I am fat.
- She **didn't use to** ride a bicycle. (Once she didn't ride a bicycle, but now she does.)
- Q: **Did** you **use to** live in Paris?
  A: **Yes**, I **did**. I **used to** live in Paris.

A Complete the sentences with the correct form of *used to* and the words in brackets.

1. _____I used to be_____ (I / be) shy, but now I'm not shy.

2. _____ (you / go) to school on foot?

3. _____ (she / live) in Korea?

4. _____ (I / not / eat) vegetables. Now I eat them every day.

5. _____ (we / ride) our bicycles, but now we take the bus.

A Look at the pictures and make sentences using *used to*, as in the example.

1.
 Past
 Now

Cindy / not be / slim
→ fat

Cindy didn't use to be slim.

She used to be fat.

2.
 Past
 Now

Olivia / not have / short hair
→ long hair

_____

_____

3.
 Past
 Now

we / not walk / to school
→ take a school bus

_____

_____

4.
Past Now

Martin and Jessica / not live / in Korea
→ in Italy

_____

_____

B Look at the pictures and read the statements. Then make questions and give short answers.

1.

Q: Did she walk to the library?

A: Yes, she did. _____ (She walked to the library.)

2.

Q: _____

A: _____ (The girls stayed at home last night.)

3.

Q: _____

A: _____ (Jada didn't finish her homework yesterday.)

C Look at the pictures. Write what these people used to do in their childhood.

1.

Jake / volleyball

→ *Jake used to play volleyball in his childhood.*

2.

Greg / a lot of pizza

→ _____

3.

Holly / glasses

→ _____

4.

Ellie / the guitar

→ _____

5.

the girls / to school

→ _____

6.

Sunny / music on the radio

→ _____

D Look at the pictures. Use the prompts to make questions and answers, as in the example.

1.

Jessica / visit / Buckingham Palace / last year / ?
→ No / visit the Louvre museum

Q: *Did Jessica visit Buckingham Palace last year?*

A: *No, she didn't. She visited the Louvre museum.*

2.

Peter / practice / the piano / last night / ?
→ No / play computer games

Q: _____

A: _____

3.

Ava and Scott / complete / the project / last week / ?
→ No / learn scuba diving

Q: _____

A: _____

A Look at the example and practice with a partner. Use the words below or invent your own. (Repeat 3 times.)

I.

What did you do this morning?

I jogged in the park.

I.

you / this morning?
→ jog in the park

2.

David / last month?
→ visit Seoul

3.

the students / this morning?
→ walk to school

4.

you / last Saturday?
→ watch TV in the afternoon and study at night

B Work with a partner. What did you use to do when you were 7 years old? Pick out ideas from the following list, then ask your partner as in the example.

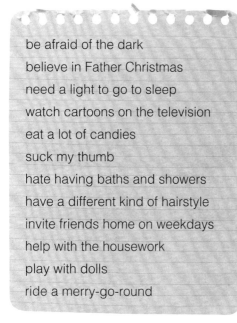

be afraid of the dark
believe in Father Christmas
need a light to go to sleep
watch cartoons on the television
eat a lot of candies
suck my thumb
hate having baths and showers
have a different kind of hairstyle
invite friends home on weekdays
help with the housework
play with dolls
ride a merry-go-round

When I was seven, I used to be afraid of the dark.

Did you use to be afraid of the dark, too?

Yes, I did.

Your turn now!

Simple Past 2

Learn & Practice

Spelling Rules of the Simple Past

- 과거 시제는 주어와 관계없이 동사 원형에 -d 또는 -ed를 붙여서 과거형을 만들어요. 일정한 규칙으로 모양이 변하지요. 우리말로 '~했(었)다'라는 뜻이에요.

대부분의 동사 → 동사 원형에 -ed를 붙임.	smell → smell**ed** walk → walk**ed** help → help**ed** cross → cross**ed** visit → visit**ed** need → need**ed**
-e로 끝나는 동사 → 동사 원형에 -d만 붙임.	arrive → arrive**d** hope → hope**d** invite → invite**d** like → like**d** love → love**d** move → move**d**
『자음+y』로 끝나는 동사 → -y를 -i로 고치고 -ed를 붙임.	study → stud**ied** cry → cr**ied** try → tr**ied** worry → worr**ied** fly → fl**ied**
『단모음+단자음』으로 끝나는 동사 → 자음을 한 번 더 쓰고 -ed를 붙임.	sto**p** → stop**ped** dro**p** → drop**ped** pla**n** → plan**ned** prefe**r** → prefer**red**

Ava **worked** in a hospital last year.
She **helped** sick people.

It **rained** yesterday.
I **needed** an umbrella.

Ⓐ Rewrite the sentences in the simple past.

1. My sister works hard. → My sister worked hard.

2. I visit France. → _____

3. They like you a lot. → _____

4. She play basketball with her friends. → _____

5. Lisa studies math with her father. → _____

6. He tries to find a taxi. → _____

Simple Past: Irregular Verbs

- 동사 원형에 -(e)d를 붙여 과거 시제를 만들지 않고 동사 자체가 과거 형태를 따로 가지고 있는 동사를 불규칙 과거 동사라고 해요.

Base Form		Past Form	Base Form		Past Form	Base Form		Past Form
buy	→	bought	sleep	→	slept	hear	→	heard
see	→	saw	teach	→	taught	sit	→	sat
go	→	went	ride	→	rode	meet	→	met
make	→	made	leave	→	left	speak	→	spoke
give	→	gave	fly	→	flew	take	→	took
have	→	had	find	→	found	drink	→	drank
come	→	came	wear	→	wore	stand	→	stood
eat	→	ate	lose	→	lost	write	→	wrote

Last Sunday Carli and Bill **went** camping in the countryside. They **found** a nice place by a river. Bill **put** up the tent.

Q: Did you **ride** the bus to school yesterday?
A: No, I didn't. I **rode** my bicycle.

A Write the simple past of these verbs.

1. go → _went_
2. sit → _____
3. sleep → _____

4. take → _____
5. make → _____
6. wear → _____

7. come → _____
8. hear → _____
9. speak → _____

B Complete the sentences with the simple past of the verbs in brackets.

1. Joe and Sunny ___went___ (go) to the beach last Saturday.

2. I _____ (buy) some books at the bookstore.

3. She _____ (drink) a cup of coffee this morning.

4. They _____ (wear) swimming suits.

Simple Past: Time Clauses with *Before* and *After*

- before, after가 '주어+동사'를 포함하여 중심 문장(main clause)을 설명해 주는 부사와 같은 역할을 할 수 있어요. 시간의 정보를 담고 있어서 시간의 부사절(time clause)이라고 합니다.
- 단독으로는 완전한 의미를 전달할 수 없고 반드시 중심 문장과 연결해야 완전한 문장이 돼요.
- 시간의 부사절은 중심 문장(주절)의 앞이나 뒤에 모두 올 수 있으며, 앞에 올 때에는 쉼표(,)를 써야 해요. 의미는 같으나 앞에 쓸 때 좀 더 강조된 표현이 돼요.

She brushed her teeth **before she went to bed**.

After I saw that horror movie, I had a nightmare.

Main Clause	Time Clause
She brushed her teeth I had a nightmare	**before she went to bed.** **after I saw that horror movie.**

Time Clause	Main Clause
Before she went to bed, **After I saw that horror movie,**	she brushed her teeth. I had a nightmare.

Ⓐ Circle the time clauses in the sentences. Then rewrite the sentences by changing the order of the clauses.

1. After we finished our homework, we took a walk.
   → We took a walk after we finished our homework.

2. He washed his face after he got up.
   → _____

3. After many people died, the war ended.
   → _____

4. I washed my hands before I had meals.
   → _____

A Read a sentence about the present, and then write a sentence about the past.

1. Nancy usually gets up at 7:00. Yesterday _____*she got up at 7:00*_____ .

2. Susan usually wakes up early. Yesterday morning _____ .

3. Bob usually walks to school. Yesterday _____ .

4. Peter usually has a sandwich for lunch. Yesterday _____ .

5. Jessica usually goes out in the evening. Yesterday evening _____ .

6. Kristen usually sleeps very well. Last night _____ .

B Look at the examples. Write sentences about yourself in the simple past with each of these verbs.

1. go ____*I went shopping with Mom last night.*____

2. watch ____*I watched an English DVD yesterday.*____

3. visit _____

4. stay _____

5. have _____

6. play _____

7. study _____

8. go _____

9. meet _____

10. drink _____

11. buy _____

C Look at the pictures. Use the prompts to make questions and answers, as in the example.

1. Christina / stay at home / two days ago / ?
   → No / go camping

   Q: Did Christina stay at home two days ago?

   A: No, she didn't. She went camping.

2. they / go to a Chinese restaurant / yesterday / ?
   → No / have lunch at home

   Q: _____

   A: _____

3. Kelly / go for a walk / in the forest / ?
   → No / go for a walk by the sea

   Q: _____

   A: _____

D Combine the two sentences into one sentence by using time clauses.

1. He asked my phone number. He left.
   → He asked my phone number before he left.
   → Before he left, he asked my phone number.

   (before)

2. We missed the last subway. We walked home.
   → _____
   → _____

   (after)

3. She did some warm-up exercises. She ran.
   → _____
   → _____

   (before)

4. They got married. They had babies.
   → _____
   → _____

   (after)

A Look at the example and practice with a partner. Use the words below or invent your own. (Repeat 3 times.)

I.

 Kevin studied for a test yesterday afternoon.

 No, he didn't study for a test. He went to the beach.

1.

Tim / study for a test yesterday afternoon
→ No / go to the beach

2.

William / clean his room last night
→ No / take out the trash

3.

Cody / eat a hamburger yesterday
→ No / roast beef

4.

Joy / wash her parent's car
→ No / babysit her sister

B Work with a partner. Ask and answer questions about what you did. Use the phrases below.

Did you watch a movie?

Yes, I did.

When did you watch it?

(I watched it) Yesterday.

Who did you watch it with?

(I watched it) With Tiffany.

How was it?

It was funny.

Your turn now!

watch a movie   wash the dishes   clean your room

help your mom/dad   study English/Korean

play tennis   talk on the phone   go to a baseball game

go camping   walk in the forest

Unit **7** Past Progressive 1

Unit Focus
- ▶ Affirmatives
- ▶ Negatives
- ▶ Yes/No Questions

Past Progressive: Affirmatives

- 과거진행 시제는 과거의 한 시점에 계속 진행 중이었던 동작을 나타내요. 우리말로 '~하고 있었다'라는 뜻이에요.

I saw you last night.
You **were waiting** for a bus.

It rained a lot last night.
It **was raining** at 11 o'clock last night.

Subject	Be Verb	Verb + -ing
I/He/She/it Tom/Mary, etc.	was	
You/We/They the boys Tom and Mary, etc.	were	sleeping.

It **was snowing** at 10:30 p.m.
I **was walking** to the park.
They **were jogging** then.
We **were riding** a roller coaster.

Ⓐ Make sentences in the past progressive.

1. I eat grapes on the dish. → *I was eating grapes on the dish.*
_____

2. They take a bath. → _____

3. She buys some movie tickets. → _____

4. My mom washes the dishes. → _____

5. Jungeun and I talk about the English class. → _____

6. He does his homework. → _____

7. Kelly has dinner with her family. → _____

Past Progressive: Negatives

- 과거진행 시제의 부정문은 be 동사(was/were) 바로 뒤에 not만 붙이면 돼요. 우리말로 '~하고 있지 않았다'라는 뜻이에요.

At 8 o'clock I **wasn't waiting** for a train.
I was listening to music.

They **weren't playing** soccer at 4:00 yesterday.
They were washing the car.

Subject	Be + Not	Verb + -ing
I/He/She/it Tom/Mary, etc.	was not (= wasn't)	working.
You/We/They the boys Tom and Mary, etc.	were not (= weren't)	

John and Carin **weren't eating** lunch.
The girl **wasn't waiting** for the school bus.
It **wasn't raining** at 7:00 yesterday morning.

Ⓐ Look at the pictures and make positives and negatives.

1.

The girls weren't walking.

The girls were running.

the girls: walk (X) / run (O)

2.

she: watch TV (X)
read a book (O)

3.

they: climb the mountain (X)
have breakfast (O)

Past Progressive: *Yes/No* Questions

- be 동사 의문문과 똑같이 be 동사의 과거형 was 또는 were를 문장 맨 앞으로 보내고 물음표를 쓰면 돼요. 대답은 yes/no로 하고 의문문에 사용한 be 동사를 이용해서 대답해요. '~하고 있었니?'라는 뜻이에요.

Q: **Was** Sophia **cleaning** the windows yesterday afternoon?
A: **Yes**, she **was**.

Q: **Were** they **dancing** at 10 o'clock yesterday morning?
A: **No**, they **weren't**. They were learning yoga.

Be Verb	Subject	Verb + *-ing*
Was	I/he/she/it Tom/Mary, etc.	**singing?**
Were	you/we/they the boys Tom and Mary, etc.	

Q: **Was** John **building** a sandcastle?
A: **Yes**, he **was**.

Q: **Were** the girls **talking** about the accident?
A: **No**, they **weren't**. They were swimming in the lake.

Ⓐ Write *yes/no* questions and complete the short answers. Use the past progressive.

1. he / go to the post office

Q: *Was he going to the post office?* A: Yes, *he was* .

2. the girl / talk to her dad

Q: _____ A: Yes, _____ .

3. they / take pictures

Q: _____ A: No, _____ .

4. Kevin / eat cookies

Q: _____ A: Yes, _____ .

5. Isabella / ride a horse

Q: _____ A: No, _____ .

6. the men / carry heavy boxes

Q: _____ A: Yes, _____ .

7. the children / sleep

Q: _____ A: No, _____ .

A Complete the questions and add a statement with the information.

1.

Kathy / sleep?
→ surf the Internet

Q: _Was Kathy sleeping_ at 10:00 last night?
A: No, she wasn't. _She was surfing the Internet._

2.

they / cry?
→ laugh

Q: _____ in the car?
A: No, they weren't. _____

3.

Peter / watch TV
→ do his homework

Q: _____ while his mother
   was away?
A: No, he wasn't. _____

4.

Karen / buy the Christmas presents
→ bake cookies

Q: _____
   at 5 o'clock yesterday?
A: No, she wasn't. _____

B What was happening in the park at 4 o'clock yesterday? What were they doing? Describe the park using the past progressive.

1. Derek / lie on the grass
   → _Derek was lying on the grass._

2. Mark / jog in the park
   → _____

3. the birds / sing on the tree
   → _____

4. Matt and Julie / sit under a tree
   → _____

5. Ethan / write his diary
   → _____

6. Joe and Amy / play badminton
   → _____

C What were you doing at the following times? Write a sentence as in the example. Use the past progressive.

1. (at 7:00 yesterday evening) _I was having dinner with my family._

2. (at 5:00 p.m. last Monday) _____

3. (at 7:00 yesterday morning) _____

4. (at 9:00 last night) _____

5. (at 4:00 p.m. last Saturday) _____

6. (at 8:00 this morning) _____

7. (an hour ago) _____

8. (half an hour ago) _____

D Look at the pictures and prompts. Ask and answer questions using the past progressive.

1.

Dad: wash / his car

Q: _What was Dad doing?_____

A: _He was washing his car._____

2.

Megan: exercise / in the gym

Q: _____

A: _____

3.

Norah: speak / on the phone

Q: _____

A: _____

4.

the women: do / some shopping

Q: _____

A: _____

5.

Paul: get / dressed

Q: _____

A: _____

6.

Lisa and Adam: take / photos

Q: _____

A: _____

A Look at the example and practice with a partner. Use the words below or invent your own. (Repeat 3 times.)

I.

 Were they walking in the forest?

 No, they weren't. They were painting the walls.

1.

they / walk in the forest?
→ No / paint the walls

2.

Mark / play tennis
yesterday morning?
→ No / have a haircut

3.

Erin / read a book
→ No / draw a picture

4.

Rick / wash the dishes
an hour ago?
→ No / do the laundry

5.

Megan / take a shower
at 8:00 this morning?
→ No / drive to work

B Work with a partner. Describe the two people in the pictures. Use the information.

	Taylor	Christina
07:00	exercise in the gym	watch TV
08:30	have breakfast	have breakfast
09:00	ride her cycle to school	go to school by car
10:00	walk to the library	study in the library
12:00	eat a salad for lunch	buy a hamburger for lunch
17:00	do her assignment	surf the Internet
19:00	have dinner	have dinner
22:00	wash the dishes after dinner	watch a DVD

Taylor

Christina

Yesterday at 07:00 Taylor was exercising in the gym and Christina was watching TV.

Yesterday at 08:30 both Taylor and Christina were having breakfast.

Your turn now!

 Unit **8** **Past Progressive 2**

⊛ **Unit Focus**
▶ Information Questions
▶ Past Progressive and Simple Past

Past Progressive: Information Questions

- 의문사가 있는 의문문은 '의문사 + was/were + 주어 + v-ing?'의 어순으로 써요. 궁금한 것을 구체적으로 물어보기 때문에 yes나 no로 대답하지 않아요.

- 의문사(who, what) 자체가 주어인 경우 '의문사(Who/What) + 동사…?'의 어순으로 써요.

Q: **What were** Kelly and Jane **doing** at 7:00**?**
A: They were jogging.

Q: **Who** was cooking**?**
A: James was (cooking).

WH- Word	Be Verb	Subject	Verb + -ing
What	was	I	saying?
Where	were	you	going?
When	was	he/she/it	working?
Why	were	you	running?
Who*	were	they	watching?

＊일상 영어에서는 whom보다 who를 더 많이 써요.

Ⓐ **Make the correct form of the past progressive.**

1. where / you / go / when / I / met / you? → *Where were you going when I met you?*

2. what / Jane / do? → _____

3. why / she / run? → _____

4. when / we / sleep? → _____

5. how / they / play? → _____

6. why / he / study / on a Saturday night? → _____

48 Unit 8

Past Progressive and Simple Past

- 과거진행 시제는 과거의 어느 특정한 시간에 어떤 행위가
진행되고 있었음을 나타낼 때 사용해요.

- 과거 시제는 이미 과거에 시작하여 과거에 그 일이 끝난
동작이나 행동을 나타내요.

Past Progressive	Simple Past

Isabella **was sleeping** at 10:00 yesterday.	Hannah first **met** her husband in 2007.

- 과거진행형과 과거 시제를 함께 쓸 경우에 이미 긴 시간 동안 진행 중이었던 동작은 과거진행형을 쓰고 나중에 짧게 일어
나 도중에 끼어든 동작은 과거 시제로 써요.

They **were having** lunch when we **arrived**.

They **were having** lunch. (longer action)
We **arrived**. (shorter action)

While Mike **was driving**, a girl **crossed** the street.

Mike **was driving**. (longer action)
A girl **crossed** the street. (shorter action)

Main Clause	Time Clause
They were having lunch A girl crossed the street	when we arrived. while Mike was driving.

Time Clause	Main Clause
When we arrived, While Mike was driving,	they were having lunch. a girl crossed the street.

A Read and choose the correct words.

1. Sandra (played / was playing) tennis yesterday.

2. Karen and Bob (helped / were helping) their mother with the housework yesterday.

3. What were you (did / doing) at 11:30 yesterday?

4. He (took / was taking) pictures at that time.

5. I (called / was calling) you lots of times, but you didn't answer the phone.

6. Christopher Columbus (arrived in / was arriving in) America in 1492.

7. Sunny (drove / was driving) to work when she crashed into a car.

8. Last night, television and radio stations (were warning / warned) about the tornado.

9. While I (washed / was washing) the dishes last night, I got a phone call from my best friend.

B Look at the pictures and fill in the blanks. Use the past progressive or the simple past of the verbs in brackets.

1.  2.

3.  4.

5.  6.

1. Jessica _____was studying_____ (study) when her mother ____arrived____ (arrive) home.

2. While Emma and Katie _____ (walk) in the park, it _____ (start) to rain.

3. When Linda _____ (have) breakfast, the doorbell _____ (ring).

4. Ron and Lisa _____ (jog) in the park when I _____ (see) them.

5. Rebecca _____ (stand) on platform 2 when her train _____ (arrive) at the station.

6. When I _____ (go) into the cafe, Sandra _____ (serve) food and drinks to the customers.

A Combine the two sentences into one sentence as in the example.

1.

I walk in the street. (longer action)
I get a phone call from my friend. (shorter action)

→ While _I was walking in the street_, _I got a phone call from my friend_ .

2.

My dad brushes his teeth. (longer action)
I arrive at home. (shorter action)

→ _____ when _____ .

3.

Susan waits for a taxi. (longer action)
It begins to rain. (shorter action)

→ While _____ , _____ .

4.

I work in the office. (longer action)
The phone rings. (shorter action)

→ While _____ , _____ .

B Write a question for each sentence. Use the *wh-* question words in brackets.

1. She was watching a DVD. (what)

   → _What was she watching?_

2. He was going to the bookstore. (where)

   → _____

3. Allison was talking to her teacher. (who)

   → _____

4. They were going to the bank this afternoon. (when)

   → _____

5. The children were playing volleyball in the park. (where)

   → _____

C Look at the pictures. Ask questions using the prompts in brackets and answer them, as in the example.

1.

Olivia / do her homework

(when / you / call / her / yesterday)

Q: *What was Olivia doing when you called her yesterday?*

A: *She was doing her homework when I called her yesterday.*

2.

Sarah / eat a hamburger

(when / you / go into a restaurant / yesterday)

Q: _____

A: _____

3.

your mother / wash the dishes

(when / you / come home / from school)

Q: _____

A: _____

4.

Jamie / shave

(when / you / see him / yesterday)

Q: _____

A: _____

D Look at the picture and write questions in the past progressive tense. The underlined words are the answers.

1. The students were looking at their teacher.

   Q: *Who were the students looking at?*

2. The students were sitting at their desks.

   Q: _____

3. They were sitting on chairs.

   Q: _____

4. They were holding their hands in the air.

   Q: _____

A Look at the example and practice with a partner. Use the words below or invent your own. (Then change roles and practice again.)

1.

 Was Nicole cooking dinner?　　 No, she wasn't cooking dinner.

 What was she doing?　　 She was speaking on the phone.

1.  Nicole / cook dinner?
→ No / speak on the phone

2.   Courtney / clean the bedroom
→ No / surf the Net

3. they / water the flowers?
→ No / watch TV

4.  Jack / write an email
→ No / play with his dog

B Work with a partner. Ask and answer questions using the information in brackets, as in the example

What were you doing at six o'clock yesterday evening?

I was doing my English homework.

Your turn now!

1. (at six o'clock yesterday evening)
→ My partner (He or She) was doing his/her English homework.
_____

2. (at half past nine last Sunday night)
→ _____

3. (at 8 a.m. this morning)
→ _____

4. (this time yesterday)
→ _____

5. (at noon last Saturday)
→ _____

The Future Tense 1

Unit Focus

▶ Future: *Be Going To*
▶ Future: *Will*
▶ *Be Going To* vs. *Will*

Future: *Be Going To*

- be going to는 마음속에 이미 하기로 결정이 되어 있는 미래의 일정(prior plan)을 나타내요. to 뒤에는 동사 원형을 쓰고 '~할 예정이다, ~하려고 한다'라고 해석해요.

- 미래의 일정이 아닌 눈앞에 뻔히 일어날 상황을 예측할 때에도 be going to를 써요.

Planned Action

We**'re going to** go to the concert next week.

Future Prediction

It**'s going to** rain. There are many dark clouds in the sky.

- be going to의 부정은 be 동사 바로 뒤에 not을 붙이기만 하면 돼요.

- be going to의 의문문은 be 동사를 문장 맨 앞으로 보내고 물음표(?)를 써 주기만 하면 돼요. 대답은 yes나 no를 사용하여 대답하면 된답니다.

Subject + *Be*	*Not Going To*	Base Verb	
I am			I**'m not going to** watch television on holiday.
He/She/It is	**not** going to	eat.	
You/We/they are			They **aren't going to** travel next week.

Be + Subject	*Going To*	Base Verb	
Am I			Q: **Is** she **going to** sell her car?
Is he/she/it	going to	go?	A: **Yes**, she **is**. / **No**, she **isn't**.
Are you/we/they			Q: **Are** they **going to** buy a new car?
			A: **Yes**, they **are**. / **No**, they **aren't**.

A Complete the sentences and check. Use *be going to* and the verbs in brackets.

	Future Prediction	Future Plan
1. She _____ (have) a picnic tomorrow.	☐	☐
2. World temperatures _____ (rise).	☐	☐

B Make questions with *be going to* and complete the short answers.

1. you / listen to music / after dinner

   Q: *Are you going to listen to music after dinner?* A: No, *I'm not* .

2. they / move / to Seattle / next summer

   Q: _____ A: Yes, _____ .

3. Linda / go / shopping

   Q: _____ A: No, _____ .

4. he / copy / this book

   Q: _____ A: Yes, _____ .

Learn & Practice 2

Future: *Will*

- will은 앞으로의 일을 단순히 예측하거나 미래의 일에 대해서 말하는 순간에 결정할 때 사용해요.
- will 뒤에는 반드시 동사 원형을 쓰고, 부정문은 will 뒤에 not을 붙여 will not(=won't)으로 써요. 일상 영어에서는 주로 won't로 써요.
- 의문문은 will을 문장 맨 앞으로 보내고 물음표(?)를 써 주면 돼요. 대답은 yes나 no로 하고 의문문에 쓰인 will을 그대로 사용해서 대답해요.

Future Prediction		**Decision at the Time of Speaking**
Scientists **will** find a cure for Parkinson's and Alzheimer's.		Q: **Will** you drive me to the station now? A: **Yes**, I **will**.

Subject	Will Not	Base Verb	
I He/She/It We/You/They	**will not** **(= won't)**	go.	I **won't** help you. They **won't** visit the zoo tomorrow. She **won't** come to the party.

Will	Subject	Base Verb	
Will	I he/she/it we/you/they	go?	Q: **Will** you arrive around five tomorrow? A: **Yes**, I **will**. / **No**, I **won't**. Q: **Will** they be at home tomorrow night? A: **Yes**, they **will**. / **No**, they **won't**.

A Write sentences. Use the future *will* and the prompts given.

1. people / live / on other planets / in the future? → Will people live on other planets in the future?

2. people / have / lots of robots / in the future. → _____

3. the weather / become / hotter / in the future? → _____

4. people / not carry / money. → _____

5. we / not get / serious diseases like cancer. → _____

Be Going To vs. Will

- 어떤 일을 하기로 결심하였거나 이미 예정된 미래의 일에는 will을 쓰지 않고 be going to를 써야 해요.
- 어떤 일을 하기로 마음에 결정하지 하지 않은 상태에서 말하는 순간에 결정한 일에는 will을 써요. be going to를 쓰면 어색한 문장이 돼요.

She's pregnant.
She**'s going to** have a baby.
NOT: She **will** have a baby.

I'm late for work!
I **will** take a taxi.
NOT: I **am going to** take a taxi.

A Complete the sentences with *will* or *be going to*.

1. A: The phone is ringing.
   B: Okay. I ____*will answer*____ (answer) it.

2. A: Look at that old woman with a big suitcase!
   B: Oh, I _____ (help) her move it!

3. A: Have you decided how to spend your summer vacation?
   B: Yeah. I _____ (stay) at home.

4. A: Do you want to go out for dinner tonight?
   B: I can't. I _____ (study) for my exams.

5. A: The laptop isn't working. I'm going to call the repairman.
   B: No, don't do that. I _____ (fix) it.

A Look at the pictures. Then complete the sentences with *be going to* and a phrase from below.

buy some vegetables   pay the bill   take a photo

have lunch   hit the puck

drink a glass of milk

1.

Luke is in the cafeteria.

He is going to have lunch.

2.

Jason is in a cafe.

_____

3.

Lisa is holding a glass of milk.

_____

4.

Brian has a hocky stick.

_____

5.

Michelle has a digital camera.

_____

6.

My parents are in the supermarket.

_____

B Choose and make sentences to respond to the statements.

clean up the trash   do the shopping   feed him

make you a sandwich   bring the equipment

1. I didn't have dinner today.   →   I will make you a sandwich.

2. The room is very dirty after the party.   →   _____

3. We don't have a CD player for the party.   →   _____

4. We don't have any food in the fridge!   →   _____

5. The puppy is hungry.   →   _____

C Look at the Parkers' schedule for next week. Write questions and answers as in the example. Use the future *be going to*.

Sunday: **Olivia** - play badminton with her dad
Monday: **Mrs. Parker** - water the plants
Tuesday: **Peter** - meet his friends
Wednesday: **Mr. Parker** - repair the car
Thursday: **Peter** - play tennis with his mom
Friday: **Mr. and Mrs. Parker** - go shopping
Saturday: **Olivia and Peter** - watch a DVD

1. Olivia / play computer games?

   Q: Is Olivia going to play computer games?

   A: No, she isn't. She's going to play badminton
   with her dad.

2. Mrs. Parker / water the plants?

   Q: _____

   A: _____

3. Peter / study math?

   Q: _____

   A: _____

4. Mr. Parker / make a cake?

   Q: _____

   A: _____

5. Peter / study in the library?

   Q: _____

   A: _____

6. Mr. and Mrs. Parker / buy a new house?

   Q: _____

   _____

   A: _____

   _____

7. Olivia and Peter / visit their aunt?

   Q: _____

   _____

   A: _____

   _____

D What are you going to do this weekend? Write what you are going to do or are not going to do on the weekend.

1. get up early   I'm going to get up early. OR I'm not going to get up early.

2. watch a movie   _____

3. do the laundry   _____

4. stay home all day   _____

5. get some exercise   _____

6. meet a friend   _____

7. do your homework   _____

8. take a long walk in the park _____

A Look at the example and practice with a partner. Use the words below or invent your own. (Then change roles and practice again.)

1.

tomorrow?
→ go shopping

1.

What are you going to do tomorrow?

I'm going to go shopping.

2.

tomorrow evening?
→ take the dog for a walk

3.

tomorrow afternoon?
→ watch a scary movie

4.

this weekend?
→ visit my grandparents

5.

tomorrow afternoon?
→ get a haircut

6.

at 9:00 tomorrow morning?
→ write an email

7.

this summer?
→ travel to Europe

B Work with a partner. William is a businessman. Look at his secretary's notes about his trip to Korea. Ask and answer questions using the prompts as in the example.

Is William going to fly at 12 o'clock on Tuesday?

No, he isn't. He's going to fly at 9 o'clock on Monday morning?

Your turn now!

Monday, October 16th
fly - 09:00 (morning)
meet - Mr. Miller - 12:00
have lunch - with Mr. Miller - 1:00

Tuesday, October 17th
make a speech - 10:00
give an interview - 3:00
fly back - 7:00

1. fly / 12:00 / Tuesday?
2. meet Mr. Miller / 12:00 / Monday?
3. have lunch with Mr. Miller / 2:00 / Monday?
4. make a speech / 11:00 / Tuesday?
5. give an interview / 5:00 / Monday?
6. fly back / 6:00 / Tuesday?

The Future Tense 2

Unit Focus

▶ *Be Going To*, Present Progressive, Simple Present
▶ Future Time Clauses
▶ Future Conditional Sentences

Learn & Practice 1

Future: *Be Going To*, Present Progressive, Simple Present

- be going to는 이미 하기로 결정되어 있는 미래의 일정(prior plan) 또는 말하는 사람의 마음과 관계없이 눈앞에 뻔히 일어날 상황을 예측할 때 써요.

- 정해진 계획과 일정에는 현재진행형이 미래를 나타낼 수 있어요. 주로 움직임을 나타내는 come, go, stay, arrive, leave 나 교통수단을 나타내는 fly, walk, ride, drive, take 등이 자주 쓰여요. 정해진 계획과 일정에 쓰는 현재진행형은 be going to와 같은 뜻이 돼요.

- 비행기/기차/영화/공연 시간표와 같이 확실히 정해진 일정에는 현재 시제가 미래를 나타내요. 단, 개인(사람)의 정해진 일정에는 현재 시제를 쓰지 않고 be going to나 현재진행형을 써야 해요.

Jane **is flying** to Singapore in two hours. (She has already arranged it.)

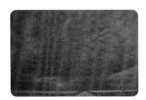

Look! It **is going to** rain. (It's certain. There are clouds in the sky, so there is visible evidence.)

The baseball game **starts** at 6:00 tomorrow. (We're talking about a timetable.)

A Complete the sentences. Use the simple progressive.

1. Q: What is Jason doing this Saturday?

   A: _He is reading a book._____ (read / a book)

2. Q: What are Jane and Tom doing this Saturday?

   A: _____ (go / to the movie theater)

B Use the prompts to make sentences.

1. the flight / leave / at 9:30 / tomorrow   → _The flight leaves at 9:30 tomorrow.___

2. the next lesson / start / at 2:00   → _____

3. the bookstore / close / at 3:00 / tomorrow   → _____

Future Time Clauses with *When, Before, and After*

- 미래를 나타내는 시간의 부사절, 즉 when, before, after가 이끄는 문장 안의 시제는 반드시 현재 시제를 써서 미래를 나타내요. will 또는 be going to를 쓰지 않아요.
- 시간의 부사절은 중심 문장과 반드시 함께 써야 완전한 의미를 전달할 수 있어요. 중심 문장의 앞에 또는 뒤에 쓸 수 있어요. 접속사(when, after, before)가 이끄는 절이 문장의 앞에 올 때에는 쉼표(,)를 써요.

After they **graduate** from university, they **will get** a good job.

When the interviewer **asks** questions, she **will answer** all of them.

Main Clause	Time Clause
They **will get** a good job	**after** they **graduate** from university.
Time Clause	Main Clause
When the interviewer **asks** questions,	she **will answer** all of them.

A Read and put the verbs in brackets into the correct tense.

1. When he ___returns___ (return), I'll give him the key.

2. She will be delighted when she _____ (hear) this.

3. Before Amy _____ (go) to work tomorrow, she will eat breakfast.

4. When we go to the park tomorrow, we _____ (go) to the zoo.

5. I _____ (get) some fresh fruit when I go to the grocery store tomorrow.

6. I will give the children their dinner before he _____ (come) home.

7. We _____ (buy) that house when we have enough money.

Future Conditional Sentences

- if는 '~한다면'이라는 뜻으로 조건을 나타내요. if가 데리고 있는 주어와 동사에서도 마찬가지로 동사에 현재 시제를 써서 미래를 표현해요. 미래를 나타내는 시제(will, be going to)를 쓸 수 없어요.
- 'if + 주어 + 동사…'만으로는 완전한 문장을 만들 수 없고 반드시 중심 문장과 함께 써야 의미를 전달할 수 있어요. 중심 문장의 앞에 또는 뒤에 모두 쓸 수 있고, if가 이끄는 절이 문장의 앞에 올 때에는 쉼표(,)를 써요.

If people **cut** trees, they **will destroy** the rainforest.

You **can see** the Eiffel Tower **if** you **go** to Paris.

If Clause (Present)	Main Clause (Future)
If people **cut** trees,	they **will destroy** the rainforest.
Main Clause (Future)	If Clause (Present)
You **can see** the Eiffel Tower	**if** you **go** to Paris.

Ⓐ Combine the two sentences as in the example.

1.

You wake the baby up.
He will cry.
→ If _you wake the baby up, he will cry._

2.

You travel to Korea.
You will meet many nice people.
→ If _____

3.

You water the plants.
They won't die.
→ If _____

4.

Cindy sometimes feels tired.
Then she listens to K-pop.
→ If _____

A Read the following sentences. Then say what these people are going to do using the words or phrases from the box.

study all day	mail it	sleep
go to the hairdresser's		take a taxi

1. Anne and Kyle are tired. _____ They are going to sleep. _____

2. William has written a letter. _____

3. Kathy has missed the bus. _____

4. Brian's hair is untidy. _____

5. Jason has an exam tomorrow. _____

B Complete the sentences with the verbs in brackets. Use the simple present or the present progressive.

1. We ____ are having ____ (have) a party next Saturday. Would you like to come?

2. I _____ (not / go) away for my vacation next month because I don't have enough money. _____ (you / go) away?

3. When the Queen _____ (arrive), the audience will stand up.

4. The concert _____ (start) at 8:00 this evening.

5. When winter _____ (begin), the swallows will fly away to a warmer country.

6. The art exhibit _____ (open) on May 3rd and _____ (close) on July 15th.

7. What time _____ (the next train / leave)?

8. Sunny, we _____ (go) to the park. _____ (you / come) with us?

9. You will see a small black box when you _____ (open) the safe.

C Look at the pictures and expand the notes into sentences. Use the words given and time clauses.

1.

Peter and Jessica / go to the movies / have / dinner after

→ Peter and Jessica will go to the movies after they have dinner.

2.

I / take a bath / get home tonight when

→ _____

3.

Tom / watch a soccer game on TV / go to bed before

→ _____

4.

Karen / wash her car / go to the gym before

→ _____

D Decide which sentence is the condition and which is the result. Then join the two sentences using if.

1. The weather will be nice tomorrow. I will go to Central Park with my friends.
   → If the weather is nice tomorrow, I will go to Central Park with my friends.

2. My mother will bake a cake. I get an A.
   → _____

3. I want to get good marks. Then my parents will be happy.
   → _____

4. I may see Aron this afternoon. I'll tell him to call you.
   → _____

5. He will be able to buy a bicycle. He saves some money.
   → _____

A Look at the example and practice with a partner. Use the words below or invent your own. (Then change roles and practice again.)

1.

 What are you going to do before you study tonight?

 Before I study tonight, I'm going to watch TV.

1.
before you study tonight?
→ watch TV

2.
after you go shopping?
→ play badminton with my mother

3.
after you finish your homework?
→ go to Central Park

4.
before you have dinner?
→ play soccer with my friends

B Work with a partner. Ask questions and answer them as in the example.

Condition: he / touch the fire?
Result: burn his hand

What will happen if he touches the fire?

If he touches the fire, he will burn his hand.

Your turn now!

Condition: she / study hard
Result: get a good test score

Condition: they / drop out of school?
Result: can't go to college later

Condition: you / spill paint on your mom's new carpet?
Result: very angry

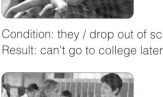

Condition: he / not do his homework
Result: get into trouble

Condition: they / watch TV late at night
Result: wake up late

Nouns and Regular Nouns

- 명사는 크게 보통명사(common noun)와 고유명사(proper noun)로 나뉘는데, 보통명사는 우리 눈에 보이는 이름을 가진 모든 명사를 말해요.

- 고유명사는 사람, 지역, 나라 등의 이름을 나타내는 특별한 명사를 말해요. 고유명사의 첫 글자는 항상 대문자로 써야 해요.

- 명사의 복수형을 만들 때에는 명사 뒤에 -s, -es, -ies 또는 -ves를 붙여서 만들어요.

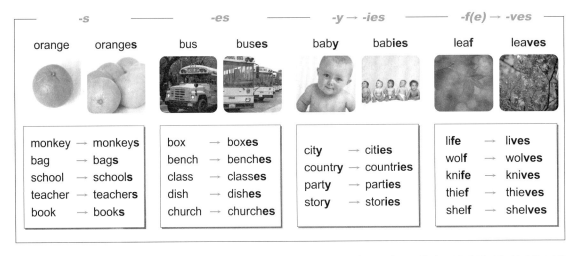

- 명사에 -(e)s를 붙이는 것처럼 일정한 규칙이 없이 자체의 복수형을 가지거나 단수와 복수형의 모양이 똑같은 불규칙 명사들도 있어요.

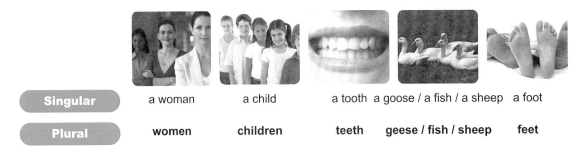

A Write the plural of the following words.

1. shelf → *shelves*　　2. goose → _____　　3. man → _____

4. box → _____　　5. dish → _____　　6. potato → _____

7. tomato → _____　　8. knife → _____　　9. city

Learn & Practice 2

Count (= Countable) and Noncount (= Uncountable) Nouns

- 셀 수 있는 명사는 단수 또는 복수 명사로 쓸 수 있어요. 단수 명사 앞에 부정관사 a를 쓰는데 명사의 첫 소리가 모음(a, e, i, o, u)일 경우에는 명사 앞에 an을 써요.

- 셀 수 없는 명사는 하나(한 명), 둘(두 명) 이렇게 수를 셀 수 없어요. 따라서 명사 앞에 부정관사 a/an을 붙일 수 없고 복수형인 -s나 -es를 붙여 복수형을 만들 수도 없어요.

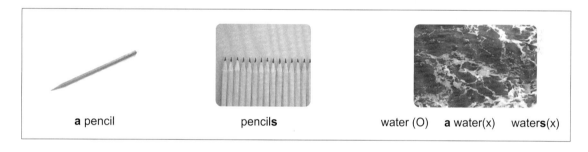

| a pencil | pencil**s** | water (O)　　**a** water(x)　　water**s**(x) |

액체	oil(기름), shampoo(샴푸)
고체	gold(금), soap(비누), silver(은), plastic(플라스틱), furniture(가구), clothing(의류)
기체	air(공기), gas(가스, 기체)
음식	food(음식), butter(버터), cheese(치즈), bread(빵), fruit(과일), water(물), juice(주스), coffee(커피), tea(차), soup(수프), milk(우유), rice(쌀), salt(소금), pepper(후추), sugar(설탕)
과목	math(수학), history(역사), English(영어), science(과학), music(음악)
운동 이름	soccer(축구), baseball(야구), basketball(농구), tennis(테니스), golf(골프), volleyball(배구)
눈에 보이진 않지만 이름이 있는 것들	help(도움), work(일), music(음악), advice(충고), information(정보), homework(숙제), happiness(행복), love(사랑), experience(경험)

- 짝을 이루어 하나를 이루는 명사는 항상 복수 명사로만 써요.

shoes　　　　glasses　　　　scissors　　　　chopsticks　　　　jeans

A Complete the sentences with the singular or plural form of the nouns.

1. Kevin has one child. Jason has two ____children____ (child).

2. The students in my class come from many _____ (country).

3. There are ten _____ (fish) in the fish bowl.

4. I like _____ (baby). They are very cute.

5. There are two _____ (goose) in the field.

6. I have to pull out some of my _____ (tooth).

Learn & Practice 3

Articles: *A/An* and *The*

- 하나, 한 명이라는 개념으로 셀 수 있는 단수 명사 앞에 a를 쓰는데, 명사의 첫소리가 모음(a, e, i, o, u)으로 발음되는 명사 앞에는 an을 써요.

- 정관사 the는 이미 언급된 명사가 반복될 때, 또는 말하는 사람이나 듣는 사람이 알 수 있는 '특정한 것'을 가리킬 때 사용해요. 특히 세상에서 유일한 자연물(the sun, the earth, etc.) 또는 악기(the piano, the violin, etc.) 앞에 the를 써요.

I can see **a** car. **The** car is red.	**The** earth travels round **the** sun.	She's playing **the** flute.	He is **a** waiter. He works in **the** restaurant.

- 과목, 스포츠, 언어, 식사, 도시, 국가를 나타내는 명사 앞에는 정관사 the를 쓰지 않아요.

Q: Did you have **breakfast?**
A: Yes, I did.

Subjects: history, science, math	Sports: soccer, basketball
Languages: English, Korean, Japanese	Meals: breakfast, lunch, dinner
Cities: Seoul, London, Beijing	Countries: France, Korea, Japan

A Write *a(n)* or *the* in the blanks. Put an X if you don't need an article.

1. Can you speak __X__ Korean?

2. Do you have _____ lunch with your friends?

3. _____ earth isn't a star. It's _____ planet.

4. She is playing _____ guitar.

5. I'm so cold. Please close _____ door.

6. _____ moon goes around _____ earth.

7. Seo-yoon speaks _____ English very well.

8. She is _____ actress.

A Write the words in plural in the correct box.

bicycle	bus	baby	knife	man	glass	child	house
apple	box	cherry	ball	tomato	ferry	leaf	tooth
goose	dress	city	wife	deer	fox	watch	
parrot	lady	wolf	dish	boy	woman	sheep	dictionary

-s	bicycles						
-es	buses						
-ies	babies						
-ves	knives						
Irregular	men						

B Look at the pictures and answer the questions about the people. Use *a* or *an*.

1.
musician

Q: What's her job?
A: She is a musician.

2.
engineer

Q: What's his job?
A: _____

3.
police officer

Q: What's his job?
A: _____

4.
doctor and nurse

Q: What are their jobs?
A: _____

5.
shop assistant

Q: What's her job?
A: _____

6.
actor and actress

Q: What are their jobs?
A: _____

C For each sentence, change the singular subject and verb to the plural.

1. You are a good friend. → _You are good friends._

2. The man is living in Hong Kong. → _____

3. The potato from the store looks yummy! → _____

4. The goose is coming to us. → _____

5. The leaf is falling from the tree. → _____

6. The watch in this shop is expensive. → _____

7. The child is playing in the garden. → _____

D In each of sentences, the definite article 'the' is missing. Rewrite each sentence to include the missing article.

1. Who is man at the door?
   → _Who is the man at the door?_

2. Neil Armstrong was first astronaut to walk on the moon.
   → _____

3. Sun rises in the east.
   → _____

4. Principal of this school has resigned.
   → _____

5. This is not book I am looking for.
   → _____

6. Were there any witnesses to accident?
   → _____

7. The soldiers had to cross desert on foot.
   → _____

A Look at the example and practice with a partner. Use the words below or invent your own. (Then change roles and practice again.)

1.

 Is there one goose in this picture?

 No, there isn't. There are three geese.

1.
one goose → three

2.
one mouse → two

3.
one lady → two

4.
one sheep → three

5.
one child → four

6.
one fish → four

7.
one patato → a lot of

8.
one bus → many

B Work with a partner. Give three pieces of information about each person, but do not say his/her name. Can your partner guess who he/she is?

He's an actor. He's from Spain. He was born in 1960.

Antonio Banderas?

Antonio Banderas - actor - Spain - born 1960

Chirstina Aguilera - singer - the USA - born 1980

Wayne Rooney - soccer player - England - born 1985

Bill Gates - businessman - the USA - born 1955

Unit 12 Quantity Words

⊛ **Unit Focus**
- ▶ Units of Measure with Nouns
- ▶ *Some* and *Any*
- ▶ *Every*
- ▶ *Many, Much, A Lot Of*

Learn & Practice 1

Units of Measure with Nouns

- 셀 수 없는 물질명사는 그 물질을 담는 그릇이나 용기를 이용하여 셀 수 있어요. 예를 들어 물은 셀 수 없지만 물을 담아 '물 한 잔, 물 두 병' 이렇게 셀 수 있는 거예요.

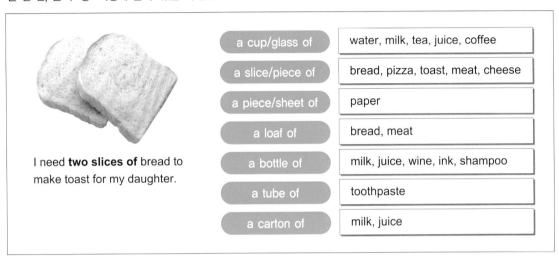

a cup/glass of	water, milk, tea, juice, coffee
a slice/piece of	bread, pizza, toast, meat, cheese
a piece/sheet of	paper
a loaf of	bread, meat
a bottle of	milk, juice, wine, ink, shampoo
a tube of	toothpaste
a carton of	milk, juice

I need **two slices of** bread to make toast for my daughter.

- '물 두 잔', '커피 세 잔'처럼 복수형으로 쓸 때에는 물질명사는 셀 수 없으므로 그대로 두고 단위를 나타내는 명사에 -(e)s 를 붙여야 해요. E.g. She drinks four cup**s** of **coffee** every day.

Ⓐ **Look at the pictures and complete the phrases.**

1.

__a loaf of__ bread

2.

_____ water

3.

_____ pizza

4.

_____ milk

5.

_____ toothpaste

6.

_____ paper

Some and *Any*

- some은 '몇몇의, 약간의, 조금'의 뜻으로 그 수나 양을 정확히 모를 때 사용해요. 단수, 복수 명사 앞에 모두 쓸 수 있고, 주로 긍정문에 써요.

- any도 '몇몇의, 약간의, 조금'의 뜻으로 어떤 수나 양을 정확히 모를 때 사용해요. 단수, 복수 명사 앞에 모두 쓸 수 있고, 주로 부정문과 의문문에 사용해요.

Susan: I want to make **some** hot dogs. I'm very hungry.
Lisa: Are there **any** sausages in the fridge?
Susan: Yes, there are **some** sausages and there's also **some** bread, but there isn't **any** cheese.

Ⓐ Complete the sentences with *a(n)*, *some*, or *any*.

1. Do you have ___any___ postcards?

2. I bought _____ cheese for my baby sister.

3. She doesn't kill _____ mosquitoes.

4. There is _____ onion on the table.

5. I need to buy _____ new car.

6. Kelly is hungry. She would like _____ food.

Every

- every와 all은 둘 다 '모든'이라는 뜻이에요. every 뒤에는 단수 명사를 쓰고 동사도 단수 동사를 써요. 반면에, all 뒤에는 복수 명사를 쓰고 동사도 복수 동사를 써야 해요.

Every student **walks** to school. = **All** the students **walk** to school.

Every student **is** happy. = **All** the students **are** happy.

Ⓐ Correct the mistakes and rewrite the sentences.

1. Every students passed the exam.   →   Every student passed the exam.

2. They studied hard every days.   →   _____

3. All Korean eats kimchi.   →   _____

4. All the child play soccer after school.   →   _____

Many, Much, A Lot Of

- many는 셀 수 있는 명사 앞, much는 셀 수 없는 명사 앞에 써요. 정확한 개수를 알 수는 없지만 막연히 '많은'이라는 뜻을 나타내요. 셀 수 없는 명사는 그 양이 아무리 많아도 단수 취급하여 동사도 단수 동사를 써야 한다는 것도 잊지 마세요.
- a lot of 또는 lots of는 '많은'이라는 뜻으로 셀 수 있는 명사와 셀 수 없는 명사 앞에 모두 쓸 수 있어요.
- how many와 how much는 '얼마나'의 뜻으로, 그 수와 양을 물어보는 말이에요. how many 뒤에는 셀 수 있는 복수 명사를 쓰고, how much 뒤에는 셀 수 없는 명사를 써요.

Q: **How much** milk does she drink?
A: She drinks **much** (= a lot of, lots of) milk.

Q: **How many** friends does she have?
A: She has **many** (= a lot of, lots of) friends.

	Affirmative	Negative	Questions
Count Nouns	There are **many** tomatoes.	There aren't **many** tomatoes.	**How many** tomatoes are there?
	There are **a lot of** onions.	There aren't **a lot of** onions.	**How many** onions are there?
	He reads **lots of** books.	He doesn't read **lots of** books.	**How many** books does he read?
Noncount Nouns	There is **much** juice.	There isn't **much** juice.	**How much** juice is there?
	There is **a lot of** cheese.	There isn't **a lot of** cheese.	**How much** cheese is there?
	She drinks **lots of** coffee.	She doesn't drink **lots of** coffee.	**How much** coffee does she drink?

A Complete the sentences using *many, much, how many,* or *how much.*

1. Did you buy __much__ food?
2. There isn't _____ rain in winter in Korea.
3. _____ sugar is there in your coffee?
4. _____ slices of pizza can you eat?
5. She doesn't buy _____ clothes.
6. Was there _____ traffic on the road?

B Choose the correct words.

1. We have (many / a lot of) milk.
2. Kelly doesn't have (a lot of / many) orange juice.
3. Kathy doesn't read (much / lots of) books.
4. Is there (much / many) snow in Singapore?
5. My mom buys (many / much) food.
6. We usually have (many / a lot of) homework.

A Use the prompts to write questions and answers, as in the example. Use *how many* or *how much*.

1. coffee / the cup → any
   Q: How much coffee is there in the cup?   A: There isn't any coffee in the cup.

2. Coke / the bottle → some
   Q: _____   A: _____

3. tomatoes / the fridge → any
   Q: _____   A: _____

4. bread / the basket → some
   Q: _____   A: _____

5. soup / the bowl → any
   Q: _____   A: _____

6. eggs / the fridge → any
   Q: _____   A: _____

B How much of these things do you eat? Use *a lot of*, *not much*, or *not many* as in the examples.

1. oranges   →   I eat a lot of oranges. _____

2. eggs   →   I don't eat many eggs. _____

3. milk   →   _____

4. tomatoes   →   _____

5. ice cream   →   _____

6. meat   →   _____

7. chocolate   →   _____

8. fruit   →   _____

9. apples   →   _____

10. pizza   →   _____

C Rewrite each sentence with *every.*

1. All the books on this desk are mine. → *Every book on this desk is mine.*

2. All the workers speak excellent French. → _____

3. All the waiters start at 8 a.m. → _____

4. All animals need oxygen like human beings. → _____

5. All the boys are playing soccer. → _____

D Read the questions and answer them as in the example.

1.

three

Q: How much milk does she drink every day?

A: *She drinks three glasses of milk.* _____

2.

seven

Q: How many slices of bread does he eat?

A: _____

3.

five

Q: How much coffee does she drink a day?

A: _____

4.

four

Q: How many pieces of pizza can he eat?

A: _____

5.

three

Q: How many cartons of milk did she buy?

A: _____

A Look at the example and practice with a partner. Use the words below or invent your own. (Then change roles and practice again.)

I.

 Is there any coffee on the table?

 Yes, there is. There is some coffee, but there aren't any tomatoes.

I.

coffee / on the table?
→ tomatoes (x)

2.

bread / on the table?
→ cherries (x)

3.

cheese / in the fridge?
→ orange juice (x)

4.

rice / in the bowl?
→ salt (x)

5.

pizza / on the table?
→ milk (x)

B Work with a partner. Ask and answer the questions with *how many* or *how much* and *are there* or *is there*.

1. movie theaters in (name of this city)
2. books in your schoolbag
3. cars in the street outside the window
4. chairs in this classroom
5. pictures in this classroom
6. museums in (name of this city)
7. milk in your refrigerator

How many students are there in this classroom?

There are 30 students.

Your turn now!

C Work with a partner. Ask and answer the questions as in the example.

1. good movie theaters
2. big museums
3. nice department stores
4. palaces
5. modern supermarkets
6. popular galleries
7. popular amusement parks

Are there any restaurants in your home town?

Yes, there are. There are a lot of good restaurants.

Your turn now!

Prepositions of Time

Unit Focus
▶ Prepositions of Time: *At, In, On*
▶ Prepositions of Time: *Before, After, For, During, Until, From...To*

Learn & Practice!

Prepositions of Time: *At, In, On*

- 시간을 나타내는 전치사 at은 구체적이고 정확한 시각 앞에 써요. at은 한 시점으로 간주되는 때를 나타내요.

We go to school **at** 8 o'clock.

Sarah watches TV **at** night.

> **At**
> **at** 6 o'clock/10:30
> **at** 11:00 a.m.
> **at** night/midnight
> **at** lunchtime
> **at** the end of...

- 시간을 나타내는 전치사 in은 달, 계절, 연도 등과 같이 비교적 긴 시간 앞에 쓰고 하루의 일부분을 말할 때에도 써요

In the summer, they go to the beach.

My mom wakes up at 6 o'clock **in** the morning.

> **In**
> **in** the morning/evening
> **in** April/May/June...
> **in** (the) summer/winter
> **in** 1999/2002...

- 시간을 나타내는 전치사 on은 날짜, 요일 그리고 하루의 일부분이 아닌 '금요일 오후'나 '일요일 밤'과 같은 특정 요일의 일부분에 써요.

Goodbye! See you **on** Friday.

They go to the movies **on** Saturday evening.

> **On**
> **on** May 25, 2012 / June 6
> **on** Wednesday
> **on** Saturday(s) / Saturday night
> **on** Friday morning
> **on** Christmas Day
> **on** the weekend (= **on** weekends)

- in은 현재를 기준으로 '지금으로부터 ~후에'라는 미래의 뜻으로도 써요. 이때는 after를 쓰지 않아요.

They will be back **in** three days.　　　　Hurry! The train leaves **in** five minutes.

A Look and write *at*, *in*, or *on*.

1.

Barack Obama, the president of the United States, was born _____ 1961

2.

I'm going to visit Angkor Wat _____ the summer.

3.

_____ Christmas Day, I will ask my parents to buy me a big present.

4.

I usually go to bed _____ 9 p.m.

5.

We celebrate New Year _____ January 1st every year.

6.

_____ the winter, the weather is very cold.

B Write the correct prepositions, *at*, *in*, or *on*.

1. The course begins ___on___ January 7th and ends ___on___ March 10th.

2. I went to bed _____ midnight and got up _____ 6:30 the next morning.

3. We traveled overnight to Paris and arrived _____ 6:00 _____ the morning.

4. I'll call you _____ Tuesday morning _____ 10:00, okay?

5. I might not be home _____ the morning. Can you call me _____ the afternoon instead?

6. Kevin's grandmother died _____ 1997 _____ the age of 79.

7. There are usually a lot of parties _____ New Year's Eve.

8. I'm just going out to do some shopping. I will be back _____ half an hour.

Prepositions of Time: *Before, After, For, During, Until, From...To*

- for와 during은 둘 다 '~ 동안에'라는 같은 뜻을 가지고 있지만 쓰임에는 차이가 있어요. for는 어떤 일이 지속된 기간을 나타내어 for 뒤에는 구체적인 기간(three days, ten years...)을 나타내는 말이 와요. 반면 during은 어떤 일이 일어난 때를 나타내어 뒤에 행사나 사건(the summer vacation, the movie) 등의 말이 와요.
- before는 '~ 전에', after는 '~ 후에'라는 뜻으로 써요.

Everybody is nervous **before** exams.

After lunch, we went shopping.

I went on vacation **for** two weeks. I visited New York **during** the summer vacation.

- until(=till)은 '~까지'의 뜻으로 어느 특정 시점까지 어떤 상태나 상황이 계속됨을 나타내요.
- from(~부터)...to(~까지)는 어떤 동작이나 상황의 시작과 끝을 나타내요.

I went to bed early. I read a book **until** 4 a.m.

Christina worked **from** 8:00 **to** 6:00 yesterday.

A Fill in the correct prepositions. Use *before, after, for, during, until*, or *from...to*.

1. There was no rain ___for___ 6 months.

2. There was no rain _____ the dry season.

3. We'll stay here _____ three days.

4. I'll stay here _____ then.

5. You should brush your teeth _____ bed

6. She will wait for you _____ 10 o'clock.

7. They visited Tokyo _____ the summer vacation.

8. Not all bears hibernate _____ the winter.

9. Alex lived in Singapore _____ eight years.

10. We lived in Canada _____ 1999 to 2005.

11. You must finish your homework _____ dinner.

12. Don't lie down right _____ a meal.

A Look at the pictures and rewrite the sentences with prepositions of time.

1.

I have my guitar lessons. (10:00 / Wednesdays)

→ I have my guitar lessons at 10:00 on Wednesdays.

2.

School starts. (8 o'clock / the morning)

→ _____

3.

We stayed in Rome. (five days)

→ _____

4.

He'll wait for you. (5 o'clock)

→ _____

5.

They go to school. (7 o'clock / the morning)

→ _____
_____

6.

They lived in Korea. (2001-2009)

→ _____
_____

B Read the questions and complete the answers as in the example.

1. Q: Did Peter watch TV for two hours last night? (three hours)
   A: No, he didn't _____. He watched TV for three hours.

2. Q: Can you wait for me until 6:00? (5:30)
   A: No, _____. _____

3. Q: Did Isabella live in Hong Kong from 2004 to 2008? (2005-2011)
   A: No, _____. _____

4. Q: Did she dance until four o'clock in the morning? (six o'clock)
   A: No, _____. _____

C Complete the text about Olivia's daily routine. Use the correct prepositions.

Olivia is a fashion designer. Her day starts _at_ seven o'clock _in_ the morning. _____ breakfast, she reads the newspaper. _____ eight o'clock she goes to work. She starts work _____ half past eight, and she finishes work _____ four o'clock _____ the afternoon.

_____ work she goes to the gym to do some exercise. _____ Wednesday afternoons she plays tennis with her friends. She goes home _____ half past five. Then she makes dinner _____ six o'clock. _____ seven o'clock she has dinner with her boyfriend. After that they normally watch TV. _____ the weekend they go to parties or go to the movies. _____ weekdays Olivia goes to bed early, _____ about ten o'clock.

D Write about your daily routine. Use the phrases on the right to help you.

I _____

_____

_____

_____

_____

_____

_____

_____

Time Expressions:
* on Mondays/ Saturday/ weekdays...
* in the morning/afternoon/ evening..
* on Sunday morning / Monday afternoons / Saturday evenings...
* on the weekend
* after breakfast/lunch/dinner
* after that / then...

E Make two sentences with *from....to/until* about things Brian did yesterday.

1. read the newspaper / 7:00 / 7:40 → He read the newspaper from 7:00 to 7:40.
   → He read the newspaper from 7:00 until 7:40.

2. have breakfast / 8:00 / 8:30 → _____
   → _____

3. wash his car / 9:00 / 10:00 → _____
   → _____

4. play badminton / 10:00 / 11:00 → _____
   → _____

5. go for a walk / 2:00 / 4:00 → _____
   → _____

A Look at the example and practice with a partner. Use the words below or invent your own. (Then change roles and practice again.)

I.

 When did Columbus arrive in America?

 He arrived in it in 1492.

I.

Columbus / arrive in / America?
→ 1492

2.

Alexander Graham Bell / invent /
the telephone?
→ 1876

3.

Neil Armstrong / land / on the moon?
→ July 20th, 1969

4.

Kim Jeongil / die?
→ 2011

B Interview! Work with a partner. Ask and answer the questions as in the example.

What time do you get up in the morning?

I usually get up at seven in the morning.

1. What time do you get up in the morning?
2. What do you like doing on the weekend?
3. What do you usually do on Saturday evenings?
4. What do you wear on a cold winter's day?
5. What time do you go to bed at night?
6. Did you go on holiday last July?
7. What do you usually do on Christmas Day?

Your turn now!

🅐 **Unit Focus**
▶ Prepositions of Place
▶ Prepositions of Movement

Prepositions of Place

- 장소를 나타내는 전치사는 명사 앞에 붙어서 사람이나 사물이 어떤 위치에 있는지를 알려 주는 역할을 해요. 전치사 in은 건물이나 구체적인 공간 안에 있을 때 또는 비교적 넓은 장소(도시, 나라) 등에 사용해요. at은 장소의 한 지점, 단체 행동이 이루어지는 구체적인 장소(회의, 파티, 콘서트 등), 또는 건물의 목적이 분명한 장소(정거장, 공항, 영화관 등)를 나타낼 때 사용해요.

Sunny is sitting **at** the bus stop.	She is **at** home now.	The Great Wall is **in** China.

- 장소를 나타내는 전치사 on은 어떤 표면에 접촉해 있는 상태거나, 버스, 기차, 비행기, 자전거, 말, 오토바이 등을 타고 있을 때 써요. 단, 자동차를 타고 있을 때에는 in a/the car, in a/the taxi처럼 in을 써요.

Look at the picture **on** the wall.	Who is the girl **on** the bicycle?	Tom and Jane are talking **in** the car.

- under(~ 아래에), behind(~ 뒤에), in front of(~ 앞에), next to / by(~ 옆에), near(~ 근처에), below(~ 아래에), above(~ 위에), opposite(~ 맞은편의, 반대쪽의)는 자주 쓰이는 장소의 전치사예요. between A and B는 (A와 B 사이에)라는 뜻이고 among 또한 '~사이에'라는 뜻이지만 between은 둘 사이, among은 셋 이상일 때 사용해요.

Amy is **under** the tree.	Tom sat down **opposite** Kathy.	The picture is **above** the sofa. The sofa is **below** the picture.

A Match to make sentences.

1. The chair is
2. The books are
3. The rulers are
4. The bag is
5. The children are
6. The picture is
7. The door is

a. in the bag.
b. behind the door.
c. next to the table.
d. under the table.
e. above the chair.
f. in front of the children.
g. on the table.

B Complete the sentences with *at*, *in*, or *on*.

1. What have you got __in__ your pocket?

2. What time do we arrive _____ Paris?

3. I saw Susan standing _____ the bus stop.

4. Her office is _____ the second floor.

5. My mom is _____ home.

6. I like to sit _____ an armchair by the fire.

7. The church has wonderful paintings _____ the ceiling.

8. Glasgow is a large city _____ Scotland.

9. Q: Where's Bob? A: He is _____ his bedroom.

10. The answer is _____ the bottom of the page.

C Look at the pictures and fill in the blanks with the correct prepositions.

1.

→ The plane flew ___*above*___ the clouds.

2.

→ The man is sitting _____ the woman.

3.

→ They are _____ the
Eiffel Tower.

4.

→ The boy is _____ his grandparents.

Prepositions of Movement

- 방향을 나타내는 전치사는 명사 앞에 붙어서 사람이나 사물이 어떤 방향으로 이동하는지를 알려 주는 역할을 해요. up(~ 위로), down(~ 아래로), into(~ 안으로), out of(~ 밖으로), through(~을 통과하여) 등의 전치사가 있어요.

The bus is going **through** the tunnel.

The man is getting **into** the taxi.
The woman is getting **out of** the taxi.

He's going **up** the hill.
She's going **down** the hill.

- 그 외에 across(~을 가로질러), along(~을 따라서), onto(~의 위로/위에), from...to[~에서(부터) ~까지], around(~ 주위에), to(~으로) 등이 자주 쓰이는 전치사예요.

The car is going **along** the street.
The man is walking **across** the street.

She's getting **onto** the plane.
The plane is going to go **from** Seoul **to** Dubai.

The birds are flying **around** the building.

They're walking **to** school.

Ⓐ Look at the pictures and write the correct prepositions.

1.

They're running ___to___ school.

2.

They're jumping _____ the pool.

3.

She's walking _____ the street.

4.

They're running _____ the hill.

5.
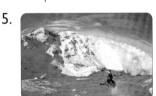
He's skiing _____ the mountain.

6.

The train came _____ the tunnel.

A Look at the picture and correct the sentences.

1. The cat is from the chair and the small table.
   → *The cat is between the chair and the small table.*

2. The schoolbag is on the table.
   → _____

3. The chair is above the bed.
   → _____

4. The sneakers are behind the bed.
   → _____

5. The books are in front of the table.
   → _____

6. The small table is above the bed.
   → _____

7. The dog is on the door.
   → _____

B Look at the pictures and make sentences with a preposition, as in the example.

1.

(they / the house / are standing)

→ *They're standing in front of the house.*

1.

(the girl / the tree / is hiding)

→ _____

3.

(the dog / Mia and Emma / is)

→ _____

4.

(they / the street / are walking)

→ _____

Prepositions of Place and Movement **87**

C Look at each picture and write the answers.

1.
2.

3.
4.

1. Q: Are they running up the hill?
   A: No, they aren't. They're running down the hill.

2. Q: Is she getting out of the bus?
   A: _____

3. Q: Is the car going around the tunnel?
   A: _____

4. Q: Is she getting into the taxi?
   A: _____

D Read and answer the questions.

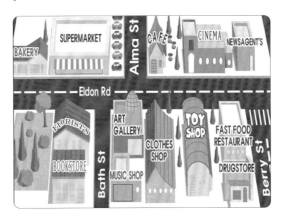

1. Q: Is there a park in your neighborhood?
   A: Yes, there is. It is opposite the bakery.

2. Q: Is there a bookstore in your neighborhood?
   A: _____

3. Q: Is there a toy shop in your neighborhood?
   A: _____

4. Q: Is there a supermarket in your neighborhood?
   A: _____

5. Q: Is there a cafe in your neighborhood?
   A: _____

A Look at the example and practice with a partner. Use the words below or invent your own. (Then change roles and practice again.)

I.

Alice / bench

I.

I'm looking for Alice. Where is she?

Over there. She is on the bench.

2.

Eric / door

3.

Tom / tree

4.

my puppy / basket

5.

Sharon / desk

6.

Anna and Kevin / house

7.

Daniel / car

B Work with a partner. Draw these things in the picture below. Don't show to your partner. Ask and describe the position of the objects using prepositions.

a book   a pencil   a cat   a pencil case   an apple   a dog   a smartphone

Where is the book?

It is under the desk.

In my picture the book is on the bed, but in your picture it is under the desk.

Your turn to ask.

⚜ **Unit Focus**

▶ *Can, could*
▶ *Should*
▶ *Must* vs. *Have To*

Learn & Practice

Can, Could

- can은 '∼할 수 있다'라는 뜻으로 현재나 미래의 능력, 허락을 나타내고, could는 '∼할 수 있었다'라는 뜻으로 과거의 능력, 허락을 나타내요. 반드시 조동사 뒤에는 동사 원형을 써야 해요. 주어가 3인칭 단수라 하더라도 동사에 -(e)s를 붙이지 않아요.

- 조동사 바로 뒤에 not을 붙여 부정문을 만들고, 의문문은 조동사(can, could)를 문장 맨 앞에 쓰고 물음표를 써요. 대답은 yes/no로 하고 의문문에 사용한 조동사를 그대로 사용합니다.

Ability

She **can** play the piano, but she **can't** play the drums.

Could he eat with chopsticks when he was a baby?

Permission

You **can't** drive a car without a licence.

You **couldn't** talk during the exam.

Subject	***Can/Could***	**Base Verb**
I/We/You He/She/It They/Tom, etc.	can/can't could/couldn't	go.

Yes/No Questions

Can you swim?	**Yes**, I **can**. / **No**, I **can't**.
Could she swim?	**Yes**, she **could**. / **No**, she **couldn't**.
Can they run?	**Yes**, they **can**. / **No**, they **can't**.

Ⓐ Complete the sentences with *can, can't, could,* or *couldn't*.

1. Sunny ___can___ play the violin really well.

2. I _____ remember her name. Do you know it?

3. We _____ go to the party because we went to a wedding.

4. Last week he _____ come to school because he was ill.

5. You _____ take your driving test until you are 18.

6. I _____ swim even when I was a baby.

7. You _____ park here. It's a bus stop.

Should

- 충고나 조언(advice, good idea)을 나타낼 때 should를 써요. '~해야 한다, ~하는 게 좋겠다'라는 뜻을 나타내요.
- 부정문을 만들 때에는 should 바로 뒤에 not을 붙여요. 우리말로 '~해서는 안 된다, ~하지 않는 게 좋겠다'라는 뜻이에요.
- 주어 앞에 should를 써서 의문문을 만들 수 있어요. 대답은 yes나 no로 하고 의문문에 사용한 조동사를 그대로 사용해서 대답해요.

You **should** eat more.
You're skinny.

You **shouldn't** watch TV
so much.

Q: **Should** I invite Tom to dinner?
A: **Yes**, you **should**.

Subject	*Should*	Base Verb	*Yes/No* Question
I/We/You He/She/It They/Tom, etc.	**should** / **shouldn't**	walk.	Q: **Should** I see a doctor? A: **Yes**, you **should**. / **No**, you **shouldn't**.

Ⓐ Complete the sentences with *should* + one of the following verbs: *eat, wear, ride.*

1.

He ___should ride___ his
bicycle very carefully.

2.

In summer weather, one
_____ sunglasses.

3.

You _____
healthy food only.

Ⓑ Complete the sentences with *should* or *shouldn't*.

1. You ___should___ do your homework every day.

2. Children _____ play with knives.

3. You _____ brush your teeth three times a day.

4. You _____ always tell the truth.

5. People _____ light fires in woods.

Must vs. *Have To*

- must와 have to는 '~해야 한다'라는 뜻으로 의무나 필요성을 나타내요. must는 상대방에게 중요성을 강조하여 선택의 여지가 없는 강한 의무나 필요성을 나타내요. 반면에, must not(=mustn't)은 '~해서는 안 된다'란 뜻으로 강한 금지를 나타내요. 주어가 3인칭 단수인 경우에는 has to를 써야 해요.

Kelly **has to** work overtime.

Every student **must** take an exam. (It's a necessity, there is no other choice.)

You **mustn't** smoke here. (It's against the law or rules.)

- have to의 부정인 don't/doesn't have to는 '~할 필요가 없다'라는 뜻으로 불필요함을 나타내요. 어떤 일에 대해 선택의 여지가 있을 때 사용해요. '~해서는 안 된다'라고 해석하면 안 돼요.
- '~해야 합니까?'라는 의문문을 쓸 때에는 do/does를 주어 앞에 쓰고 물음표(?)를 써요.

Today is Sunday. You **don't have to** get up early.

Q: **Do** we **have to** work on Saturday?
A: **Yes**, you **do**. / **No**, you **don't** (have to).

Ⓐ Look at the signs and write what you must or must not do.

1.
swim here
→ You must not swim here.

2.
stop
→ _____

3.
use a cell phone
→ _____

4.
turn left
→ _____

Ⓑ Make questions with *Do/Does...have to...?*

1. you / learn Korean → *Do you have to learn Korean?*

2. Mary / take an exam → _____

3. the children / walk home → _____

92 Unit 15

A Read the following library rules. Make sentences with *must* or *mustn't*.

Library Rules
- Do not smoke in the library.
- Do not run in the hallway.
- Do not make any noise.
- Do not eat in the library.
- Be careful with the books.
- Do not leave your phone on the tables when you leave.
- Put the books back in the right place.

1. You must not smoke in the library.

2. _____

3. _____

4. _____

5. _____

6. _____

7. _____

B Mother is telling her son what he should or shouldn't do. Write sentences as in the example.

1. He is late for school.
   → You shouldn't be late for school.

2. He comes home late.
   → _____

3. He doesn't do his homework.
   → _____

4. He doesn't clean his room.
   → _____

5. He's not nice to his brother and sister.
   → _____

C Read the following instructions. Then write sentences with *must*, *must not*, or *don't have to*, as in the examples.

1. It's necessary to fasten your seat belt throughout the flight.
   → You must fasten your seat belt throughout the flight.

2. It is forbidden to smoke in a public place.
   → You must not smoke in a public place.

3. It isn't necessary to buy a new TV set.
   → _____

4. It isn't necessary to wear a suit to the office.
   → _____

5. It isn't necessary to wear safety glasses.
   → _____

6. It is necessary to clean the living room every week.
   → _____

7. It is forbidden to touch statues in the museum.
   → _____

D Write questions and answer them about yourself using *Can you...?*

1. write with your left hand
   Q: Can you write with your left hand?   A: Yes, I can. / No, I can't.

2. eat with chopsticks
   Q: _____   A: _____

3. ride a snowboard
   Q: _____   A: _____

4. make a kite
   Q: _____   A: _____

5. sing in another language
   Q: _____   A: _____

6. play a musical instrument
   Q: _____   A: _____

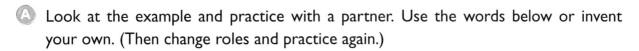

A Look at the example and practice with a partner. Use the words below or invent your own. (Then change roles and practice again.)

1.

the dog / is ill
→ take it / to the vet

I.

The dog is ill.

You should take it to the vet.

2.

I / have a headache
→ take an aspirin

3.

the milk / smells bad
→ not drink it

4.

I / feel very tired
→ take a break

5.

the water / is very dirty
→ not swim here

B Work with a partner. Make sentences using *must*, *mustn't*, or *don't have to*.

- two things you must do every day
- two things you don't have to do at home
- two things you must do at school / in class
- two things you mustn't do at school / in class

I must do my homework every day. I don't have to bring my lunch.

Your turn now!

C Imagine that you are an interviewer. Ask your partner about things he or she can do.

1. play a musical instrument
2. play a sport
3. speak three or four languages
4. ride a bicycle
5. what kind of food / cook
6. what sports / play
7. write with your left hand
8. fix things around your house

Can you ride a bicycle?

Yes, I can.

Your turn to ask now!

Unit **16** Helping Verbs 2

Unit Focus
▶ *May/Might/Can/Could* to Express Possibility
▶ *May/Could/Can I* to Ask for Permission
▶ *Would/Could/Can You* to Make Requests
▶ *Must* to Make Deductions

Learn & Practice 1

May, Might, Can, and *Could* to Express Possibility

- 어떤 일이 일어날 가능성에 대한 확신이 없을 때(50% 이하)에는 may, might, could를 써요. '～일지 모른다'라는 뜻으로 가능성을 나타내요. can은 특정한 상황이 아닌 일반적인 가능성을 나타낼 때 주로 써요.
- 어떤 일에 대한 가능성을 나타내는 의문문에는 may를 쓰지 않아요. might는 너무 격식을 갖추는 표현이 되어 잘 쓰지 않고 could를 자주 씁니다.

It **may/might/could** rain tomorrow.
(= Perhaps it will rain tomorrow.)

You **can** get stamps from the local newsagents.

Could she pass the exam?
Might she pass the exam?
(very formal)

Subject	Modal (+ *Not*)	Base Verb
I/We/You He/She/It They/Tom, etc.	**may** **may not** **might** **might not** **could**	go.

* may not, might not은 축약형을 쓰지 않아요.
* 가능성을 나타내는 표현에선 could의 부정형인 could not을 쓰지 않아요.
  I **may/might** not go to work tomorrow.
  ~~I could not go to work tomorrow.~~ (X)

Ⓐ Rewrite the sentences with *may, might,* or *could.*

1. Perhaps Sarah is ill. → *Sarah may/might/could be ill.*
2. Perhaps we won't go out. → *We may/might not go out.*
3. Perhaps it won't rain. → _____
4. Perhaps we'll buy a car. → _____
5. Perhaps Kevin isn't at home. → _____
6. Perhaps Ann needs help. → _____
7. Perhaps Heather won't change her job. → _____

96 Unit 16

May I, Could I, Can I to Ask for Permission

- I를 주어로 써서 May/Could/Can I...?로 정중한 부탁(polite request)을 표현할 수 있어요. May I...?가 가장 정중한 표현이고, 일상에서는 Could I...?를 가장 많이 쓰고, 친구나 가족과 같이 편안한 사이에서는 Can I...?를 써요

- 긍정의 대답은 Yes., Yes, of course., Certainly., Sure., No problem., Okay. 등을 쓰고 부정의 대답은 I'm sorry, but... 또는 No, I'm sorry. 뒤에 이유를 말해요. No.로만 대답하면 어색하고 무례하다고 생각할 수 있습니다.

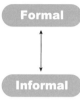

Formal
May I use your dictionary?
(They don't know each other.)
Could I use your dictionary?
(They might or might not know each other.)
Can I use your dictionary?
(They have been speaking together, or they know each other.)
Informal

A Look at the pictures. Complete the sentences with *may I*, *could I*, or *can I*. There is more than one correct answer.

1.

May/Could I see your boarding pass, please?

2.

_____ use your cell phone?

3.

_____ hand in my homework tomorrow?

Would You, Could You, and Can You to Make Requests

- you를 주어로 써서 Would/Could/Can you...?로 정중한 부탁(polite request)을 표현할 수 있어요. 가족이나 친구 등과 같이 편한 사이에서는 Can you...?를 가장 자주 써요.

- 긍정의 대답은 Sure., Certainly., OK., Yes, of course. 등으로, 부정의 대답은 I'm sorry, but I can't...나 I'd like to, but I don't... 등으로 상황에 알맞은 이유를 말해요.

Q: **Would/Could you** meet me later?
A: Yes, of course.

Q: **Can you** drive me to the library, Dad?
A: Sure.

A **Rewrite the sentences with the words in brackets.**

1. I want you to pass me the sugar. (could)
   → Could you pass me the sugar?

2. I want you to give me directions to the city hall. (would)
   → _____

3. I want you to look over this report. (could)
   → _____

4. I want you to wash the dishes for me. (can)
   → _____

Learn & Practice 4

Must to Make Deductions

- 100% 현재의 사실이라고 확신할 때에는 현재형을 쓰고, '~임에 틀림없다'라는 뜻으로 어떤 상황에 대한 논리적 근거를 토대로 강한 확신(95%)을 나타낼 때에는 must (be)를 써요. must는 '~해야 한다'라는 강한 의미를 나타낸다는 것도 잊지 마세요.

A: I'm looking for Cindy. Do you know where she is?
B: She **is** in the library. (100% certainty)
   She **must be** in the library. (95% certainty)
   She **may/might/could** be in the library. (less than 50% certainty)

A **Complete the sentences with *must* or *must not* of the verbs in brackets.**

1. Kimberly ___must be___ (be) hurt. She just fell off the ladder.

2. They _____ (be) twins. They are absolutely identical.

3. Amy plays tennis every day. She _____ (like) to play tennis.

4. Brian ate everything on his plate except the pickle. He _____ (like) pickles.

5. Somebody is knocking on the door. It _____ (be) Kathy. She went to a party.

6. William is always at home on Friday. He _____ (work) then.

7. The restaurant _____ (be) very good. It's always full of people.

A Make sentences with *Would/Could you...?* or *Can you...?* as in the examples.

1. Ask your teacher to help you with the exercise.
   → Would/Could you help me with the exercise?

2. Ask your brother to help you with the exercise.
   → Can you help me with the exercise?

3. Ask the lady to fasten her seat belt.
   → _____

4. Ask your boss to open the door.
   → _____

5. Ask your friend to tell you the time.
   → _____

6. Ask the waitress to bring you some water.
   → _____

B Talk about possible happenings. Make sentences as in the example.

1. Do you think it will rain this afternoon? (may)
   → It may rain this afternoon.

2. Do you think Karen will come to the party? (might not)
   → _____

3. Do you think Eric will be late? (may not)
   → _____

4. Do you think Nancy will pass the exam? (might)
   → _____

5. Do you think they'll be waiting for us? (may not)
   → _____

6. Do you think the plane will crash? (might not)
   → _____

7. Do you think Steve will have an accident? (might)
   → _____

C Make polite questions with *May/Could I...?* or *Can I...?* Use the verbs in brackets.

1. You're speaking to your brother.
   Lend me your dictionary. → (borrow) Can I borrow your dictionary?

2. You're speaking to a waiter.
   I want a glass of water. → (have) _____

3. You're speaking to your boss.
   I'm leaving early today. → (leave) _____

4. You're speaking to your teacher.
   I want to hand in my homework next week. → (hand in) _____

5. You're speaking to your sister.
   I'm going to turn on the TV. → (turn on) _____

6. You're speaking to a stranger.
   I'll put my coat here. → (put) _____

D Read the situations. Use the words in parentheses to write sentences with *must* or *must not*.

1. The restaurant is always empty.
   → The restaurant (= It) must not be very good. _____ (be / very good)

2. Ruth does the same thing every day.
   → _____ (get very bored / with her job)

3. Brian knows a lot about movies.
   → _____ (like / to go to the movies)

4. Their car isn't outside their house.
   → _____ (be / home)

5. They haven't lived here very long.
   → _____ (know / many people)

6. I wonder why Susan isn't at work today.
   → _____ (be / sick)

7. Max seems to know a lot about history.
   → _____ (read / a lot of books)

A Look at the example and practice with a partner. Use the words below or invent your own. (Then change roles and practice again.)

1.

What are you going to do tomorrow night?

I'm not sure. I may/might go downtown.

1.
tomorrow night?
→ go downtown

2.
this evening?
→ stay home

3.
tomorrow afternoon?
→ have lunch with Isabella

4.
tomorrow night?
→ watch a movie

5.
this evening?
→ do my homework

B Work with a partner. Your partner is an assistant in a coffee shop. You are a customer. Order food and drink. Here's the menu:

Coffee
Espresso
Black coffee
White coffee
Cappuccino
Iced coffee

Drink
Mineral water
Orange juice

Food
Green salad
Chicken salad
Cheese salad
Chicken sandwich
Cheese sandwich

What can I do for you?

Can I have an espresso, please?

Of course. Anything else?

No, thanks.

For here or takeout?

For here, please. / Takeout, please.

 **Unit 17** **Infinitives**

**Unit Focus**
- ▶ Verb + Infinitive
- ▶ Verb + Object + Infinitive
- ▶ Infinitive of Purpose

Learn & Practice

Verb + Infinitive

- study(공부하다)를 to study(공부하는 것), eat(먹다)을 to eat(먹는 것)이라고 하는 것처럼 우리말 '~하는 것(을)'이란 의미로 동작이나 행위의 표현을 늘리기 위해 동사 앞에 to를 붙인 'to + v(동사 원형)'을 to 부정사라고 해요.
- 일반적으로 동사의 목적어로 명사나 대명사를 쓰지만 동작이나 행동을 나타낼 때에는 동사 뒤에 to 부정사를 써요. 부정사는 현재나 앞으로 해야 할 행동을 내포하고 있으므로 다음과 같은 동사들 뒤에는 부정사를 써요.

want	expect	need	decide	hope
would like	plan	promise	would love	wish
like	begin	start		

I like Korean.
I like it.
I like **to study** Korean.

We want a horror movie.
We want it.
We want **to see** a horror movie.

My dad promised **to buy** a car for me.

Ⓐ **Complete the sentences as in the example.**

1. like / play computer games
   → Tom _____ likes to play computer games _____.

2. need / sleep
   → I'm very tired. I _____.

3. decided / go to Singapore
   → She _____.

4. would like / have some orange juice
   → We _____.

Verb + Object + Infinitive

- 목적어에 있는 어떤 사람이 동작이나 행동을 하길 원할 때 목적어 뒤에 부정사를 써서 '동사 + 목적어 + to 부정사'로 나타내요. 이때 부정사는 목적어(사람)가 '앞으로 해야 할 현재나 미래의 일'을 내포하고 있으므로 주로 충고나 명령에 관련된 동사와 함께 부정사를 자주 써요.

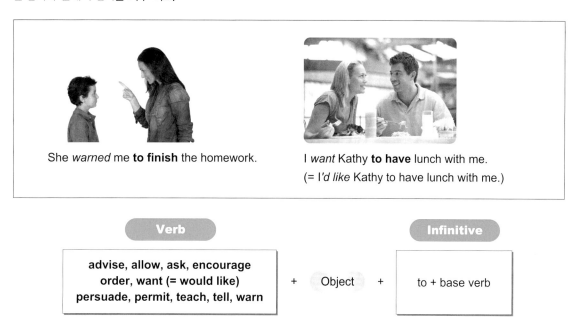

She *warned* me **to finish** the homework.

I *want* Kathy **to have** lunch with me.
(= I'*d like* Kathy to have lunch with me.)

Verb		**Infinitive**
advise, allow, ask, encourage order, want (= would like) persuade, permit, teach, tell, warn	+ Object +	to + base verb

Ⓐ Fill in the table below. Write the verb, the object, and the infinitive for each underlined phrase.

1. She told Karen to eat more vegetables.
2. She advised me to stop smoking.
3. Sally often asks Nancy to drive her home from school.
4. He asked her to stand up.
5. I expect you to rewrite the report.
6. The teacher ordered students to clean the classroom.

	Verb	Object	Infinitive
1.	told	Karen	to eat
2.			
3.			
4.			
5.			
6.			

Infinitive of Purpose

- 부정사는 동사의 구체적인 목적이나 이유를 나타낼 수 있어요. 우리말로 '～하기 위하여'라는 뜻이에요. '～하기 위하여'라는 뜻으로 in order to를 쓰기도 하는데 일상 영어에서는 in order를 거의 쓰지 않고 to 부정사만 써요.
- '～하기 위하여'라는 뜻의 to 부정사를 'for + 명사'로 써서 목적을 나타낼 수 있어요.

Q: Why did William go to the airport?
A: He *went* to the airport **to meet** his friend.

We *go* to the cafeteria **to have** lunch.
= We *go* to the cafeteria **for** lunch.

Jane *goes* jogging every morning **(in order) to keep** healthy.

Ⓐ Read and choose the correct words.

1. She saved much money (to / for) buy a new bike.

2. They're going to the supermarket (to / for) milk and bread.

3. We went to the restaurant (to / for) dinner.

4. We need a listening book (to / for) learn listening skills.

5. Kevin is going to the grocery store (to / for) some vegetables.

6. They're going to Brazil (to / for) see their friends.

Ⓑ Complete the sentences. Choose from the box.

> to see who it was   to buy some books   to watch the news
> to learn Korean   to study economics

1. I turned on the television _____to watch the news_____.

2. I'd like to go to Seoul _____.

3. The doorbell rang, so I looked out the window _____.

4. Peter wants to go to college _____.

5. She went to the bookstore _____.

A Look at the pictures and complete the sentences. Begin with the words given.

1.
> Susan, you should invite Fred to the party.

Susan's friend wants *her to invite Fred to the party*.

2.
> Someday I'll be a famous doctor. That's my dream.

Emily wants _____
_____.

3.
> No, Sejin, you can't use my smartphone.

Jisu won't allow _____
_____.

4.
> I'm bored with this job. I'm going to find a new one.

Helen decided _____
_____.

5.
> Brad, you should exercise every day.

The doctor advised _____
_____.

6.
> You must finish your homework, girls.

The teacher ordered ____
_____.

B Where did you go yesterday? Why did you go to these places? Make sentences as in the example. Use the phrases in the box.

buy some clothes	eat a hamburger	mail some letters
see a movie	buy some books	reserve a flight

1. the post office → I went to the post office to mail some letters.

2. a fast food restaurant → _____

3. the bookstore → _____

4. the travel agency → _____

5. a movie theater → _____

6. the department store → _____

C What do your parents want you to do/be in life?

1. My parents want me to be a teacher. _____
2. _____
3. _____
4. _____

D Complete the sentences for each situation.

1. It's late. Let's take a taxi. — OK, fine.

→ They decided _____ to take a taxi _____ .

2. Can you lend me some money? — Sure.

→ The man agreed _____ .

3. Please brush your teeth after meals. — I will. I promise.

→ Her daughter promised _____
_____ .

E Why did Jennifer do the following things? Match and write sentences as in the example.

1. go to Pizza Hut
2. go to the library
3. turn up the volume
4. send an email to Steve
5. buy a magazine

• why: invite him / to a party
• why: have / dinner
• why: read an article / about her favorite K-pop star
• why: hear / the news better
• why: borrow / a book

1. Jennifer went to Pizza Hut to have dinner. _____
2. _____
3. _____
4. _____
5. _____

A Look at the example and practice with a partner. Use the words below or invent your own. (Then change roles and practice again.)

1.

 Why did Kathy go to the library?

 She went to the library to borrow some books.

1.
Lauren / go to the library?
→ borrow / some books

2.
Tom / go to the swimming pool?
→ swim

3.
Michael / cross his middle and index fingers?
→ wish good luck

4.
Cindy / wear glasses
→ look intelligent

5.
Robert / go to the airport?
→ see off his friend

6.
they / go to the theater?
→ see the Phantom of Opera

B Work with a partner. Say what your parents (don't) allow or (don't) want you to do using the prompts below.

- watch TV late at night
- tidy my room
- become a doctor/teacher
- become a lawyer/singer
- walk alone at night
- improve my behavior
- study hard
- invite friends home
- go to a party on the weekend
- have breakfast every morning
- oversleep
- eat junk food
- read a newspaper
- brush my teeth after meals

My parents don't allow me to watch TV late at night.

My parents want me to become a doctor.

Unit **18** **Gerunds**

Unit Focus

▶ Gerunds: Subject
▶ Gerunds: Object
▶ *Go + -ing*

Gerunds: Subject

- 동명사는 부정사와 마찬가지로 동작의 표현을 늘리기 위해 만들어졌어요. 동사에 –ing를 붙여 명사처럼 주어 또는 목적어 자리에서 동작을 나타내요. study(공부하다)를 studying(공부하는 것), eat(먹다)을 eating(먹는 것)으로 쓰는 것처럼 동작을 가진 명사라고 하여 동명사라고 불러요.

- 주어 자리에 명사나 대명사를 쓰지만 동작의 내용을 주어 자리에 쓸 때 동명사(v-ing)를 써요. 우리말로 '~하는 것, ~하기(는)'라는 뜻이 돼요.

Noun	**Korean history** is very interesting.
Pronoun	**It** is very interesting.
Gerund	**Learning** Korean history is very interesting.

A Underline the subjects and check the correct blanks.

1. Eating too much is bad for health.　　　　　Noun: ____　Pronoun: ____　Gerund: ____

2. Speaking in English is not easy.　　　　　Noun: ____　Pronoun: ____　Gerund: ____

3. The subway is crowded with people.　　　　Noun: ____　Pronoun: ____　Gerund: ____

4. My dog gave birth to three puppies yesterday.　Noun: ____　Pronoun: ____　Gerund: ____

5. She called me while I was asleep.　　　　　Noun: ____　Pronoun: ____　Gerund: ____

B Complete the sentences using the prompts given, as in the example.

1. _____Learning a foreign language_____ (learn a foreign language) is important.

2. _____ (take the subway) is much faster than driving.

3. _____ (get up early in the morning) is tough.

4. _____ (speak English well) will be very helpful.

5. _____ (swim in the sea) can be dangerous for children.

Gerunds: Object

- 동사의 목적어로 명사나 대명사를 쓰지만 동작이나 행동을 표현할 때에는 동명사를 써요. '~하는 것(을)'이라는 뜻으로 해석해요.
- 동명사는 과거에 한번 경험했거나 기억을 가지고 있는 행위를 내포하고 있기 때문에 다음과 같은 특정한 동사 뒤에 동명사를 써야 해요. 부정사를 쓰지 않도록 조심해야 해요.

Why do you *dislike* **living** in Seoul?

She *enjoys* **listening** to K-pop music.

Verb		Object
enjoy finish give up keep mind avoid stop put off quit dislike	+	verb + -ing

- 다음과 같은 동사들은 목적어로 동명사와 to 부정사를 모두 목적어로 쓰고 그 의미도 똑같아요.

It **started raining**.
= It **started to rain**.

She **likes singing**.
= She **likes to sing**.

Verb		Gerund/Infinitive
like hate love begin start continue	+	**to + base verb** *or* **verb + -ing**

Ⓐ Complete the sentences with the gerund or infinitive form of the verbs in brackets. Sometimes two answers are possible.

1. Justin, would you mind ___mailing___ (mail) this letter on your way home?

2. At last I finished _____ (prepare) for the final exam.

3. Do you expect _____ (pass) this course?

4. Why do you keep _____ (ask) me the same question over and over again?

5. I'm planning _____ (go) to Chicago next week.

6. It started _____ (snow) around midnight.

7. She loves _____ (go) with her friends.

Go + -ing

- 'go + -ing'는 우리말로 '~하러 가다'라는 뜻으로 운동이나 레저 활동을 나타내는 말로 자주 써요. go와 동명사(-ing) 사이에 to를 쓰지 않도록 조심하세요.

Let's **go** snowboard**ing** this weekend.

If you want to **go** shopp**ing** in Seoul, Insa-dong is a great choice.

Go	-ing
go	camping
	fishing
	shopping
	hiking
	jogging
	bowling
	sightseeing
	sailing
	skating
	swimming

A Look at the pictures and complete the sentences. Use *go/goes* + *-ing*.

1.

shop

Sunny _____goes shopping_____ every Saturday.

2.

swim

Tomorrow, we'll _____ .

3.

ski

Do you _____ every winter?

4.

camp

Children likes to _____ .

A Write sentences with the gerund of the verbs in brackets.

1. Math is not easy. (study)

→ Studying math is not easy.

2. Rocks is dangerous. (climb)

→ _____

3. Some rest is the most important thing. (get)

→ _____

4. A language means learning another culture. (learn)

→ _____

5. Energy is good for our environment. (save)

→ _____

B Match and make sentences as in the example.

1.

He •   • avoided •   • eat dinner

2.

She •   • finished •   • smoke

3.

They •   • stopped •   • answer my phone

4.

I •   • enjoyed •   • listen to music

1. He stopped smoking. _____   2. _____

3. _____   4. _____

C What do you like to do in your free time? Write three things with *go* + *-ing*. Use some of the phrases in the box.

go shopping	go fishing	go dancing
go swimming	visit friends	watch TV
surf the Net	go camping	go snowboarding

1. In my free time, I like going shopping. I also like going fishing with my father.

2. _____

3. _____

4. _____

D Read about four students. Complete the sentences as in the example.

	Sean	Kate	Joshua	Shannon
things the person enjoyed	play the drums	jog with her father	ride a bicycle	eat healthy food
things the person will stop	fight with his brother	eat junk food	play computer games	watch soap operas

1. Sean enjoyed playing the drums .

   Sean will stop fighting with his brother .

2. Kate _____ .

   Kate _____ .

3. Joshua _____ .

   Joshua _____ .

4. Shannon _____ .

   Shannon _____ .

A Look at the example and practice with a partner. Use the words below or invent your own. (Then change roles and practice again.)

1.

 When you have free time, what do you like doing?

 I love reading comic books.

1.
read / comic books

2.
go / shop with my mother

3.
ride / a bicycle near the river

4.
watch / soap operas

5.
make / model airplanes

B Work with a partner. Look at the leisure activities. Ask and answer these questions.

- What do you like doing?
- How often do you do this leisure activity?
- What don't you like doing?
- What do you want to do this evening?
- What do you want to do this Saturday and Sunday?

What do you like doing?

I like reading a book.

How often do you do this leisure activity?

I usually read a book in the evening.

go to the theater

play soccer

read a book

eat out

go for a walk

play tennis

watch TV

ride a bicycle

go swimming

go sightseeing

do exercise

Unit **19** **Need & Want / Would Like**

Unit Focus
- ▶ *Need* and *Want*
- ▶ *Would Like*
- ▶ *Would Like* vs. *Like*

Learn & Practice 1

Need and Want

- need는 '∼이 필요하다'라는 말이고, want는 '∼을 원하다'라는 말이에요. 또, need는 어떤 것이 반드시 필요하다는 강한 어조를 담고 있고, want는 어떤 것을 갖길 원하나 반드시 필요하지는 않다는 의미를 담고 있어요.
- need와 want 뒤에는 목적어로 명사 또는 부정사(to + 동사 원형)를 목적어로 가질 수 있어요. 부정사는 우리말로 '∼하는 것(을)'이라는 뜻으로 해석하면 돼요.

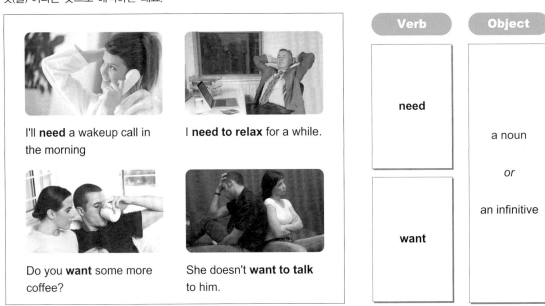

I'll **need** a wakeup call in the morning

I **need to relax** for a while.

Do you **want** some more coffee?

She doesn't **want to talk** to him.

Verb	Object
need	a noun *or* an infinitive
want	

Ⓐ **Answer the following questions using the phrases in brackets.**

1. Q: What do you need?
   A: I need some water. _____ (some water)

2. Q: What does he want?
   A: _____ (a new dictionary)

3. Q: What do they need to do?
   A: _____ (go to school)

4. Q: What does he want to do?
   A: _____ (travel around the world)

5. Q: What do you need to do?
   A: _____ (eat breakfast)

Would Like

- would like와 want는 둘 다 '~을 원하다'라는 같은 뜻을 가지고 있어요. 다만 would like가 want보다 정중한(공손한) 표현이에요.
- would like 뒤에는 목적어로 명사나 부정사(to + 동사 원형)를 쓸 수 있고, 부정문에는 would 바로 뒤에 not을 붙여요. 의문문에는 would를 문장 맨 앞으로 보내고 물음표를 써요. 대답은 yes/no로 답해요.

I want a milkshake.
I'd like a milkshake.

Affirmative Statements

Subject	*Would Like*	Object
I/You We/They He/She/Mary, etc.	would like (='d like) / wouldn't like	a noun *or* an infinitive

I **would like to** leave a message.
I **wouldn't like to** leave a message.

Q: **Would** you **like to** leave a message?
A: **Yes**, I **would**. / **No**, I **wouldn't**.

Yes/No Questions

Would	Subject	*Like*	Object
Would	you/he/she they	like	some water? / to go?

Short Answers

Yes,	No,
I/we **would**.	I/we **wouldn't**.
he/she **would**.	he/she **wouldn't**.
you **would**.	you **wouldn't**.
they **would**.	they **wouldn't**.

＊의문문을 만들 때 *Would I...?*와 *Would we...?*는 잘 사용하지 않아요.

Ⓐ Make affirmative and negative sentences. Use *would like*.

1. I / a cup of tea

    A: I'd like a cup of tea. _____   N: I wouldn't like a cup of tea. _____

2. She / go to the theater

    A: _____   N: _____

3. They / learn Chinese

    A: _____   N: _____

B Make *yes*/*no* questions and complete the short answers.

1. I'd like a sandwich.

Q: *Would you like a sandwich?*

A: Yes, *I would* .

2. She'd like a glass of water.

Q: _____

A: No, _____ .

3. I'd like to have a pet.

Q: _____

A: Yes, _____ .

4. Tony'd like to see a movie tonight.

Q: _____

A: No, _____ .

Would Like vs. Like

- like는 특정한 상황이 아닌 일반적으로 좋아하거나 즐기는 것, 즉 선호하는 것을 말할 때 써요. like 뒤에 목적어로 명사 또는 부정사를 쓸 수 있고, 동명사를 써도 의미에 큰 차이가 없어요.

- would like는 현재나 미래의 어떤 특정한 상황에서 원하는 것을 말할 때 써요. would like 뒤에 목적어로 명사 또는 부정사는 쓸 수 있지만 동명사는 쓸 수 없어요.

I **would like** to go to the zoo.
(*I would like to go to the zoo* means I want to go to the zoo.)

I **like** to go to the zoo.
(*I like to go to the zoo* means I enjoy the zoo.)

A Complete the sentences using *like* + *to* infinitive or *would like* + *to* infinitive with the verbs in brackets.

1. My aunt is very fat. She ___*would like to lose*___ (lose) some weight.

2. Eddie _____ (swim) in the pool in summer. He goes every day.

3. My brother _____ (eat) carrots. He couldn't live without them.

4. She _____ (go) to bed now. She's tired.

5. I _____ (go) home earlier than usual today. I have an appointment with the doctor.

A Complete the dialogs with *would like* or *would like to*.

1. A: I _____would like_____ two hamburgers and a small Coke.
   B: OK. For here or to go?

2. A: _____ you _____ join our debate club?
   B: Yes, I'd love to.

3. A: Which color would you like to try on?
   B: I _____ try on the pink one.

4. A: What would you like to do tonight?
   B: I _____ watch the movie on TV.

5. A: _____ you _____ some ice cream?
   B: No, thank you.

6. A: What kinds of toppings would she like?
   B: She _____ ham and tomato.

B Complete the questions with *do you like* or *would you like*.

1. Q: _____Would you like_____ to go to the movie theater tonight? A: Yes, I'd love to.

2. Q: _____ to watch horror movies?
   A: No, I don't. I prefer romantic comedies.

3. Q: _____ a cup of coffee? A: Yes, please. With milk and sugar.

4. Q: _____ to learn Korean? A: Yes, I do. I love learning Korean.

5. Q: _____ to study history? A: Yes, I do. It's very interesting.

6. Q: _____ some soup? A: No, thanks. I don't like soup.

7. Q: _____ to go to Sydney?
   A: Oh yes, I'd love to. I want to see the Opera House.

8. Q: _____ to do the housework? A: No, I don't. It's boring.

C Answer these questions using *I like, I would like, or I need.*

1. What do you like to watch on television?
   → I like to watch the news. _____ (the news)

2. Where would you like to go to study English?
   → _____ (Canada)

3. What do you need to do tomorrow morning?
   → _____ (go to school at 7:00)

4. Where would you like to go on vacation?
   → _____ (Switzerland)

5. What do you like to do in your free time?
   → _____ (go fishing with my father)

6. Where wouldn't you like to live?
   → _____ (in an apartment)

D Look at the pictures and prompts. Write questions and answers as in the example.

1.
you / become a
doctor?
→ No / a teacher

Q: Would you like to become a doctor?
A: No, I wouldn't. I'd like to become a teacher.

2.
Tom / learn
Japanese?
→ No / Korean

Q: _____
A: _____

3.
you / have a
motorcycle?
→ No / a smartphone

Q: _____
A: _____

4.
Melissa / go to
Japan?
→ No / Egypt

Q: _____
A: _____

A Look at the example and practice with a partner. Use the words below or invent your own. (Then change roles and practice again.)

1.

 Where would you like to go on vacation?

 I'd like to go to Sydney to see the Opera House.

1.
Sydney
→ the Opera House

2.
San Francisco
→ the Golden Gate

3.
Australia
→ Ayers Rock in the desert

4.
Scotland
→ the Loch Ness Monster

5.
London
→ Buckingham Palace

6.
New York
→ Central Park

B Work with a partner. Ask questions and answers as in the example.

JOBS

architect

police officer

doctor

florist

ballerina (ballerino)

teacher

magician

pilot

photographer

artist

musician

hairdresser

farmer

cook

veterinarian/vet

What kind of job would like to do in the future?

I'd like to become a doctor because I want to help sick people.

Your trun to ask now!

Unit 20 Comparison

Unit Focus
▶ Comparatives
▶ Spelling Rules: Adjectives, Adverbs
▶ *As...As* and *Not As...As*

Learn & Practice

Comparatives

- 두 명의 사람 또는 두 개의 사물(동물)을 놓고 서로 비교하는 말을 비교급이라고 해요. 우리말에는 '더 ~하다'라는 말을 붙여 쓸 수 있지만 영어에는 이렇게 정해진 말이 없어요. 그래서 형용사나 부사의 끝에 보통 -er을 붙여서 각각 '더 ~한', '더 ~하게'라는 의미를 나타내고 '~보다'라는 의미의 than을 비교하는 대상 앞에 써서 비교급을 만들어요.

Comparative: Adjective + *-er than* ——— Comparative: Adverb + *-er than*

The Mississippi is a long river.
The Nile is long**er than** the Mississippi.

A train is fast.
A plane is fast**er than** a train.

Ⓐ Complete the sentences with *-er than* of the words in brackets.

1.

A soccer ball is ___*bigger than*___ (big) a baseball.

2.

The cheetah is _____ (fast) the deer.

3.

The boy is _____ (tall) the girl.

4.

Athens is _____ (old) Rome.

Spelling Rules: Adjectives

	Adjective	Comparative	Adjective	Comparative
형용사의 음절이 1음절이면 -er을 붙여요. -e로 끝나는 단어는 -r만 붙이면 돼요.	tall	taller	slow	slower
	small	smaller	short	shorter
	nice	nicer	cheap	cheaper
'단모음+단자음'으로 끝날 때에는 마지막 자음을 한 번 더 쓰고 -er을 붙여요.	big	bigger	thin	thinner
	fat	fatter	hot	hotter
'자음+-y'로 끝나면 -y를 -i로 바꾸고 -er을 붙여요.	easy	easier	heavy	heavier
	pretty	prettier	happy	happier
2음절 이상의 형용사는 형용사 앞에 more를 써요.	famous	more famous	expensive	more expensive
	interesting	more interesting	difficult	more difficult

Spelling Rules: Adverbs

	Adverb	Comparative	Adverb	Comparative
-ly로 끝나는 부사 앞에는 more를 붙여요.	slowly	more slowly	quickly	more quickly
	loudly	more loudly	beautifully	more beautifully
-ly로 끝나지 않는 부사는 -(e)r을 부사 뒤에 붙여요.	fast	faster	hard	harder
	late	later		

＊예외: early의 비교급은 more를 붙이지 않고 -y를 지우고 -ier을 붙여서 earlier로 만들어요.

Ⓐ Write the comparative form of each word.

1. pretty → _prettier_
2. busy → _____
3. hot → _____
4. slowly → _____
5. big → _____
6. thin → _____
7. cheap → _____
8. fast → _____
9. expensive → _____
10. old → _____
11. long → _____
12. famous → _____
13. late → _____
14. easy → _____
15. tall → _____
16. heavy → _____
17. difficult → _____
18. quickly → _____
19. fat → _____
20. cold → _____
21. happy → _____

As...As and Not As...As

- 두 명의 사람 또는 두 개의 사물이 서로 같거나 비슷하다고 표현하는 말을 원급 비교라고 해요. 형용사/부사에 -er을 붙이지 않은 원래 형태(원급)를 이용하여 as + 형용사/부사 + as와 같이 써요.
- 첫 번째 as는 큰 뜻이 없고 두 번째 as는 우리말로 '~만큼'이라고 해석하면 돼요.
- 부정문인 'not as + 형용사/부사 + as'는 두 번째 as만 해석하여 '~만큼 ~하지 않다'라는 뜻이에요. 또, 'not as...as'는 '-er than'의 비교급 형태로 바꾸어 쓸 수 있어요.

Eric   Brian

Eric and Brian are twins.

Eric is **as** *old* **as** Brian. (They are the same age.)

Eric is **as** *tall* **as** Brian. (They are the same height.)

Eric isn**'t as** *smart* **as** Brian.

= Brian is smart**er than** Eric.

A Complete the sentences with *as* or *than*.

1. Ashley is older ___than___ Kelly.

2. He isn't as intelligent _____ his brother.

3. Belgium is smaller _____ Switzerland.

4. Soda pop isn't as healthy _____ fruit juice.

5. Listening to music is as interesting _____ watching TV.

6. She studied harder _____ me.

7. Kristen is _____ tall as Martin.

8. Brandi wasn't as busy _____ Erika.

B Change the sentences as in the example. Use *not as...as*.

1. My mother is older than my father.   →   My father isn't as old as my mother.

2. Thailand is hotter than Korea.   →   _____

3. Physics is more difficult than history.   →   _____

4. The Amazon is longer than the Nile.   →   _____

A Look at the information and write sentences about Ava and Rachel. Compare the two girls using the following adjectives.

Ava
95 pounds (43 kilos)
5 feet (153 centimeters)
quiet
13 years old

Rachel
115 pounds (52 kilos)
5 feet 4 inches (165 centimeters)
friendly
14 years old

1. old   Rachel is older than Ava.

2. light

3. heavy

4. short

5. tall

6. quiet

7. friendly

B Rewrite or join the following sentences using *as...as* or *not as...as*.

1. I was very tired. Stacey was very tired.

→ I was as tired as Stacey.

2. The Han River is not so clean. The Amazon is clean.

→

3. Listening to K-pop music is interesting. Watching DMB TV is interesting, too.

→

4. A river isn't big. An ocean is very big.

→

5. I didn't study very hard. Rosie studied very hard.

→

C Complete each sentence as in the example.

1. Lisa is prettier than Claire.

   as   →   Claire is not _____*as pretty as*_____ Lisa.

2. Meat isn't as healthy as vegetables.

   than   →   Vegetables are _____ meat.

3. The math test wasn't that difficult.

   as   →   The math test wasn't _____ I expected.

4. Betty is 79 years old. Graham is 79 years old, too.

   old   →   Betty is _____ Graham.

5. Your bag is very light like a feather.

   light   →   Your bag is _____ a feather.

6. This necklace costs $100. That necklace costs $200.

   expensive   →   That necklace is _____ this one.

D Look at the information and complete the sentences about London and New York. Compare the two cities using the words below.

London
Population: 6.7 million
Temperatures: 4-18℃
Rain: 1,123 mm

New York
Population: 8.0 million
Temperatures: 1-23℃
Rain: 610 mm

1. crowed   New York is more _____*crowded than*_____ London.

2. **hot**   The summer in New York is _____ the summer in London.

3. **rainy**   London is _____ New York.

4. **tall**   The buildings in New York are _____ the buildings in London.

5. **modern**   The buildings in New York are _____ the buildings in London.

6. **fast**   Life in New York is _____ life in London.

A Look at the example and practice with a partner. Use the words below or invent your own. (Then change roles and practice again.)

1.

Is China as big as Canada?

No, Canada is bigger than China.

1.
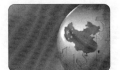
China: big as Canada?
→ No / than China

2.

English: difficult as Korean?
→ No / than English

3.

a turtle: fast as a cheetah?
→ No / than a turtle

4.

the earth: big as the sun?
→ No / than the earth

5.

science: complex as philosophy?
→ No / than science

6.

the Atlantic Ocean: deep as the Pacific Ocean?
→ No / than the Atlantic Ocean

B Work with a partner. You and your partner recently visited two different family restaurants. Look at the information below and compare the two restaurants, as in the example.

Outback Steakhouse

Bennigan's

The Bennigan's is larger than the Outback Steakhouse.

Your trun now!

	Outback Steakhouse	Bennigan's
large	★	★★
expensive	★★	★
healthy	★★	★
convenient	★	★★
comfortable	★	★★
old	★★	★
crowded	★	★★
modern	★★	★
exciting	★	★★

You are my

Grammar & Speaking

(2)
Workbook

Answer Key

Unit 1
Simple Present
p. 6

Learn & Practice 1

A **1.** Kevin wakes up early in the morning.

   2. Jane goes to work at 8:00.

   3. They love their country.

   4. Wilson takes the children to the beach.

B **1.** doesn't go   **2.** doesn't help   **3.** don't need

   4. don't start

Learn & Practice 2

A **1.** sleeps   **2.** watches   **3.** copies   **4.** finishes   **5.** stays

   6. enjoys   **7.** washes   **8.** has   **9.** says

B **1.** We   **2.** He   **3.** My dad   **4.** I   **5.** Bread   **6.** She

   7. That child   **8.** All those buses

Learn & Practice 3

A **1.** Q: Does she play the guitar well?   A: she does

   2. Q: Does he have a pet?   A: he doesn't

   3. Q: Do they speak Chinese?   A: they do

   4. Q: Does the sun give us energy?   A: it does

Learn & Practice 4

A **1.** begins (Future)   **2.** leaves (Future)   **3.** takes (Habit)

Super Writing

A **1.** The movie starts at 10:00 tomorrow morning.

   2. Tom's plane arrives at 11:00 tomorrow morning.

   3. The soccer game begins at 8:00 p.m. tomorrow.

   4. What time does the baseball game begin

       tomorrow?

B Peter studies hard and swims very well, but he doesn't

    ride a bicycle or listen to K-pop music.

    Isabella rides a bicycle and listens to K-pop music, but

    she doesn't study hard or swim very well.

    Tina and Ben study hard and ride a bicycle, but they

    don't swim very well or listen to K-pop music.

C **1.** Q: How often does Tom take out the trash?

       A: He takes out the trash once a week.

   2. Q: What does Scott do on Saturday mornings?

       A: He washes his car.

   3. Q: How often do you study Korean?

       A: I study Korean four times a week.

   4. Q: Where does Jessica go every day?

       A: She goes to school.

D **1.** Q: Does Nancy live in Seattle?

       N: Nancy doesn't live in Seattle.

   2. Q: Does she take a bus to work?

       N: She doesn't take the bus to work.

   3. Q: Do Mike and Lee read a lot of newspapers?

       N: Mike and Lee don't read a lot of newspapers.

   4. Q: Do they speak on the phone a lot?

       N: They don't speak on the phone a lot.

   5. Q: Does Jennifer have classes every day?

       N: Jennifer doesn't have classes every day.

Unit 2
Present Progressive
p. 12

Learn & Practice 1

A **1.** is sitting (Right Now)   **2.** is eating (Right Now)

   3. am studying (Around Now)

   4. is working (Around Now)

   5. are taking (Around Now)   **6.** is playing (Right Now)

Learn & Practice 2

A

walk → walking	ride → riding	cut → cutting
playing	writing	swimming
working	making	stopping
reading	coming	sitting
eating	loving	running

B **1.** is working   **2.** are listening   **3.** is making

   4. are eating

Learn & Practice 3

A **1.** Q: Is she buying the striped shirt?   A: she is

   2. Q: Is it raining outside?   A: it isn't

   3. Q: Are they shopping now?   A: they are

   4. Q: Are you wearing your new blouse?   A: I'm not

   5. Q: Is she smiling at me?   A: she isn't

   6. Q: Is he staying in a hotel near the sea?   A: he is

Super Writing

A **1.** → The baby is crying loudly.

      → He isn't sleeping.

2. → Lucy isn't watching TV.

   → She is talking on the phone.

3. → Eric is running on a track.

   → He isn't playing the violin.

4. → Ava and Peter aren't having lunch.

   → They are seeing a scary movie.

B 1. They're playing with their baby Steve.

2. They're playing in the park.

3. He is wearing a T-shirt and pants.

4. Bob is wearing a hood.

5. Nancy is holding the baby's arm.

C 1. Q: Are the boys playing soccer?

   A: No, they aren't. They are playing basketball.

2. Q: Is your sister working on her computer now?

   A: No, she isn't. She is having lunch.

3. Q: Is Jessica reading a comic book?

   A: No, she isn't. She is studying math.

4. Q: Is scott washing the car now?

   A: No, he isn't. He is doing the laundry.

D 1. The man and the woman aren't standing in the street. They are sitting in a car.

2. The man isn't working on a laptop. He is speaking on the phone.

3. The woman isn't speaking on the phone. She is working on a laptop.

4. It isn't raining. The sun is shining.

5. The man isn't holding a wallet. He is holding a phone.

Unit 3

Simple Present vs. Present Progressive p. 18

Learn & Practice 1

A 1. drinks 2. isn't raining 3. speaks 4. is stealing

5. has 6. is waiting

Learn & Practice 2

A 1. am always losing 2. is always playing

3. are always watching 4. is always complaining

Learn & Practice 3

A 1. present 2. future 3. future 4. future 5. present

6. present 7. future 8. present 9. future 10. future

Super Writing

A 1. usually gets up at 7:30 every day, but today she is still sleeping

2. usually has breakfast at 8:30 every day, but today she is watching TV

3. usually drives to work at 9:00 every day, but today she is walking in the park

4. usually learns yoga at 6:00 every day, but today she is making dinner

B 1. She's having lunch with John

2. She's attending a meeting

3. She's going to the dentist

4. She's giving a presentation to her boss

5. She's going to Peter and Susan's house for dinner

6. She's meeting Lisa outside the movie theater

7. She's playing tennis with Nancy

C 1. Q: What does Jeffrey usually do in the evenings?

   A: He usually stays at home.

2. Q: What are Tom and Paul doing this evening?

   A: They are playing a board game.

3. Q: What does Sandra usually eat for breakfast?

   A: She usually eats toast and jam.

4. Q: What is Jennifer doing now?

   A: She is drinking orange juice.

D 1. is always taking 2. is always barking

3. are always laughing 4. is always talking

5. is always missing 6. is always eating

Unit 4

The Verb Be p. 24

Learn & Practice 1

A 1. was; am 2. was; is 3. is; was 4. are; were

5. was; is

Learn & Practice 2

A 1. She wasn't angry at me.

2. I'm not at home right now.

3. Jane wasn't very tired last night.

4. Our room isn't very big, and it isn't very clean.

5. The history books aren't interesting.

6. Grace and Karen weren't my classmates.

7. Ten years ago, Jerry wasn't in fifth grade.

Learn & Practice 3

A 1. Q: Are you hungry? A: I am
   2. Q: Was Mozart a musician? A: he was
   3. Q: Was Thomas Edison a painter? A: he wasn't
   4. Q: Was Michael Jackson a singer? A: he was
   5. Q: Is he a basketball team coach? A: he isn't
   6. Q: Are your parents young? A: they are

Super Writing

A 1. No, she isn't. She is an actress.
   2. No, she isn't. She is 32 years old.
   3. Yes, he is.
   4. No, he isn't. He is from the USA.
   5. No, she isn't. She is 20 years old.
   6. No, he isn't. He is a photographer.
   7. No, they aren't. They are 32 years old.
   8. No, he isn't. He is a student.

B 1. is; are; was; were 2. is; are; were 3. is; is; was

C 1. Q: Was Elvis Presley a politician?
      A: No, he wasn't. He was a very famous singer.
   2. Q: Was James Dean an architect?
      A: No, he wasn't. He was a very famous actor.
   3. Q: Was Van Gogh an engineer?
      A: no, he wasn't. He was a very famous painter.
   4. Q: Were Alexander Graham Bell and Thomas Edison musicians?
      A: No, they weren't. They were very famous inventors.

D 1. Q: Is Harry a teacher?
      A: No, he isn't. He is a police officer.
   2. Q: Is Isabel a soccer player?
      A: No, she isn't. She is a tennis player.
   3. Q: Are they plumbers?
      A: No, they aren't. They are mechanics.
   4. Q: Are Susan and Dylan detectives?
      A: No, they aren't. They are doctors.

Unit 5
Simple Past 1
p. 30

Learn & Practice 1

A 1. Harry didn't work last Sunday.
   2. I didn't play hockey yesterday.
   3. We didn't finish the project last night.
   4. They didn't stay at a hotel last week.
   5. It didn't rain a lot here yesterday.
   6. Bill didn't cook the potatoes yesterday.

Learn & Practice 2

A 1. Q: Did she visit the Natural History Museum?
      A: she didn't
   2. Q: Did he travel by helicopter? A: he did
   3. Q: Did Tom and Jane like tea and cookies?
      A: they didn't
   4. Q: Did the students watch the NBC show?
      A: they did
   5. Q: Did Kathy walk in Central Park this morning?
      A: she didn't
   6. Q: Did Brian enjoy the trip in Egypt? A: he did

Learn & Practice 3

A 1. I used to be 2. Did you use to go
   3. Did she use to live 4. I didn't use to eat
   5. We used to ride

Super Writing

A 1. Cindy didn't use to be slim. She used to be fat.
   2. Olivia didn't use to have short hair. She used to have long hair.
   3. We didn't use to walk to school. We used to take a school bus.
   4. Martin and Jessica didn't use to live in Korea. They used to live in Italy.

B 1. Q: Did she walk to the library? A: Yes, she did.
   2. Q: Did the girls stay at home last night?
      A: Yes, they did.
   3. Q: Did Jada finish her homework yesterday?
      A: No, she didn't.

C 1. Jake used to play volleyball in his childhood.
   2. Greg used to eat a lot of pizza in his childhood.
   3. Holly used to wear glasses in her childhood.
   4. Ellie used to play the guitar in her childhood.
   5. The girls used to walk to school in their childhood.
   6. Sunny used to listen to music on the radio in her childhood.

D 1. Q: Did Jessica visit Buckingham Palace last year?
      A: No, she didn't. She visited the Louvre museum.
   2. Q: Did Peter practice the piano last night?
      A: No, he didn't. He played computer games.
   3. Q: Did Ava and Scott complete the project last week?

A: No, they didn't. They learned scuba diving.

Unit 6
p. 36
Simple Past 2

Learn & Practice 1
A 1. My sister worked hard.
 2. I visited France.
 3. They liked you a lot.
 4. She played basketball with her friends.
 5. Lisa studied math with her father.
 6. He tried to find a taxi.

Learn & Practice 2
A 1. went 2. sat 3. slept 4. took 5. made 6. wore
 7. came 8. heard 9. spoke
B 1. went 2. bought 3. drank 4. wore

Learn & Practice 3
A 1. We took a walk after we finished our homework.
 2. After he got up, he washed his face.
 3. The war ended after many people died.
 4. Before I had meals, I washed my hands.

Super Writing
A 1. she got up at 7:00 2. she woke up early
 3. he walked to school 4. he had a sandwich for lunch
 5. she went out 6. she slept very well
C 1. Q: Did Christina stay at home two days ago?
   A: No, she didn't. She went camping.
 2. Q: Did they go to a Chinese restaurant yesterday?
   A: No, they didn't. They had lunch at home.
 3. Q: Did Kelly go for a walk in the forest?
   A: No, she didn't. She went for a walk by the sea.
D 1. → He asked my phone number before he left.
   → Before he left, he asked my phone number.
 2. → After we missed the last subway, we walked
    home.
   → We walked home after we missed the last
    subway.
 3. → She did some warm-up exercises before she ran.
   → Before she ran, she did some warm-up exercises.
 4. → After they got married, they had babies.
   → They had babies after they got married.

Unit 7
p. 42
Past Progressive 1

Learn & Practice 1
A 1. I was eating grapes on the dish.
 2. They were taking a bath.
 3. She was buying some movie tickets.
 4. My mom was washing the dishes.
 5. Jungeun and I were talking about the English class.
 6. He was doing his homework.
 7. Kelly was having dinner with her family.

Learn & Practice 2
A 1. The girls weren't walking. The girls were running.
 2. She wasn't watching TV. She was reading a book.
 3. They weren't climbing the mountain. They were
    having breakfast.

Learn & Practice 3
A 1. Q: Was he going to the post office? A: he was
 2. Q: Was the girl talking to her dad? A: she was
 3. Q: Were they taking pictures? A: they weren't
 4. Q: Was Kevin eating cookies? A: he was
 5. Q: Was Isabella riding a horse? A: she wasn't
 6. Q: Were the men carrying heavy boxes?
    A: they were
 7. Q: Were the children sleeping? A: they weren't

Super Writing
A 1. Q: Was Kathy sleeping
    A: She was surfing the Internet.
 2. Q: Were they crying A: They were laughing.
 3. Q: Was peter watching TV
    A: He was doing his homework.
 4. Q: Was Karen buying the Christmas presents
    A: She was baking cookies.
B 1. Derek was lying on the grass.
 2. Mark was jogging in the park.
 3. The birds were singing on the tree.
 4. Matt and Julie were sitting under a tree.
 5. Ethan was writing his diary.
 6. Joe and Amy were playing badminton.
D 1. Q: What was Dad doing?
    A: He was washing his car.
 2. Q: What was Megan doing?
    A: She was exercising in the gym.

3. Q: What was Norah doing?

A: She was speaking on the phone.

4. Q: What were the women doing?

A: They were doing some shopping.

5. Q: What was Paul doing?

A: He was getting dressed.

6. Q: What were Lisa and Adam doing?

A: They were taking photos.

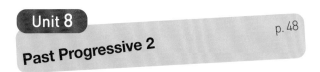

Unit 8
Past Progressive 2
p. 48

Learn & Practice 1

A **1.** Where were you going when I met you?

2. What was Jane doing?

3. Why was she running?

4. When were we sleeping?

5. How were they playing?

6. Why was he studying on a Saturday night?

Learn & Practice 2

A **1.** played **2.** helped **3.** doing **4.** was taking

5. called **6.** arrived in **7.** was driving **8.** warned

9. was washing

B **1.** was studying; arrived

2. were walking; started

3. was having; rang

4. were jogging; saw

5. was standing; arrived

6. went; was serving

Super Writing

A **1.** While I was walking in the street, I got a phone call from my friend.

2. My dad was brushing his teeth when I arrived at home.

3. While Susan was waiting for a taxi, it began to rain.

4. While I was working in the office, the phone rang.

B **1.** What was she watching?

2. Where was he going?

3. Who was talking to her teacher? / Who was Allison talking to?

4. When were they going to the bank?

5. Where were the children playing volleyball?

C **1.** Q: What was Olivia doing when you called her

yesterday?

A: She was doing her homework when I called her yesterday.

2. Q: What was Sarah doing when you went into a restaurant yesterday?

A: She was eating a hamburger when I went into a restaurant yesterday.

3. Q: What was your mother doing when you came home from school?

A: She was washing the dishes when I came home from school.

4. Q: What was Jamie doing when you saw him yesterday?

A: He was shaving when I saw him yesterday.

D **1.** Who were the students looking at?

2. Who was sitting at their desks?

3. Where were they sitting?

4. Where were they holding their hands?

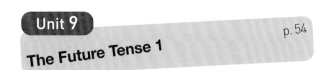

Unit 9
The Future Tense 1
p. 54

Learn & Practice 1

A **1.** is going to have (Future Plan)

2. are going to rise (Future Prediction)

B **1.** Q: Are you going to listen to music after dinner?

A: I'm not

2. Q: Are they going to move to Seattle next summer?

A: they are

3. Q: Is Linda going to go shopping? A: she isn't

4. Q: Is he going to copy this book? A: he is

Learn & Practice 2

A **1.** Will people live on other planets in the future?

2. People will have lots of robots in the future.

3. Will the weather become hotter in the future?

4. People won't carry money.

5. We won't get serious diseases like cancer.

Learn & Practice 3

A **1.** will answer **2.** will help **3.** am going to stay

4. am going to study **5.** will fix

Super Writing

A 1. He is going to have lunch.

2. He is going to pay the bill.

3. She is going to drink a glass of milk.

4. He is going to hit the puck.

5. She is going to take a photo.

6. They are going to buy some vegetables.

B 1. I will make you a sandwich.

2. I will clean up the trash.

3. I will bring the equipment.

4. I will do the shopping.

5. I will feed him.

C 1. Q: Is Olivia going to play computer games?

A: No, she isn't. She's going to play badminton with her dad.

2. Q: Is Mrs. Parker going to water the plants?

A: Yes, she is.

3. Q: Is Peter going to study math?

A: No, he isn't. He's going to meet his friends.

4. Q: Is Mr. Parker going to make a cake?

A: No, he isn't. He's going to repair the car.

5. Q: Is Peter going to study in the library?

A: No, he isn't. He's going to play tennis with his mom.

6. Q: Are Mr. and Mrs. Parker going to buy a new house?

A: No, they aren't They're going to go shopping.

7. Q: Are Olivia and Peter going to visit their aunt?

A: No, they aren't. They're going to watch a DVD.

2. you travel to Korea, you will meet many nice people.

3. you water the plants, they won't die.

4. Cindy sometimes feels tired, then she listens to K-pop.

Super Writing

A 1. They are going to sleep.

2. He is going to mail it.

3. She is going to take a taxi.

4. He is going to go to the hairdresser's.

5. He is going to study all day.

B 1. are having 2. am not going; Are you going

3. arrives 4. starts 5. begins 6. opens; closes

7. does the next train leave

8. are going; Are you coming 9. open

C 1. Peter and Jessica will go to the movies after they have dinner.

2. I will take a bath when I get home tonight.

3. Tom will watch a soccer game on TV before he goes to bed.

4. Karen will wash her car before she goes to the gym.

D 1. If the weather is nice tomorrow, I will go to Central Park with my friends.

2. If I get an A, my mother will bake a cake.

3. If I get good marks, my parents will be happy.

4. If I see Aron this afternoon, I'll tell him to call you.

5. If he saves some money, he will be able to buy a bicycle.

Unit 10
The Future Tense 2

p. 60

Learn & Practice 1

A 1. He is reading a book.

2. They are going to go to the movie theater.

B 1. The flight leaves at 9:30 tomorrow.

2. The next lesson starts at 2:00.

3. The bookstore closes at 3:00 tomorrow.

Learn & Practice 2

A 1. returns 2. hears 3. goes 4. will go 5. will get

6. comes 7. will buy

Learn & Practice 3

A 1. you wake the baby up, he will cry.

Unit 11
Nouns and Articles

p. 66

Learn & Practice 1

A 1. shelves 2. geese 3. men 4. boxes 5. dishes

6. potatoes 7. tomatoes 8. knives 9. cities

Learn & Practice 2

A 1. children 2. countries 3. fish 4. babies 5. geese

6. teeth

Learn & Practice 3

A 1. X 2. X 3. The; a 4. the 5. the 6. The; the 7. X

8. an

Super Writing

A

-s	-es	-ies	-ves	Irregular
bicycles	buses	babies	knives	men
houses	glasses	cherries	leaves	children
apples	boxes	ferries	wives	teeth
balls	tomatoes	cities	wolves	geese
parrots	dresses	ladies		deer
boys	foxes	dictionaries		women
	watches			sheep
	dishes			

B 1. She is a musician.

2. He is an engineer.

3. He is a police officer.

4. They are a doctor and a nurse.

5. She is a shop assistant.

6. They are an actor and an actress.

C 1. You are good friends.

2. The men are living in Hong Kong.

3. The potatoes from the store look yummy!

4. The geese are coming to us.

5. The leaves are falling from the tree.

6. The watches in this shop are expensive.

7. The children are playing in the garden.

D 1. Who is the man at the door?

2. Neil Armstrong was the first astronaut to walk on the moon.

3. The sun rises in the east.

4. The principal of this school has resigned.

5. This is not the book I am looking for.

6. Were there any witnesses to the accident?

7. The soldiers had to cross the desert on foot.

Unit 12
Quantity Words
p. 72

Learn & Practice 1

A 1. a loaf of 2. two glasses of 3. three pieces/slices of 4. three cartons of 5. a tube of 6. a sheet/piece of

Learn & Practice 2

A 1. any 2. some 3. any 4. an 5. a 6. some

Learn & Practice 3

A 1. Every student passed the exam.

2. They studied hard every day.

3. All Koreans eat kimchi.

4. All the children play soccer after school.

Learn & Practice 4

A 1. much 2. much 3. How much 4. How many 5. many 6. much

B 1. a lot of 2. a lot of 3. lots of 4. much 5. much 6. a lot of

Super Writing

A 1. Q: How much coffee is there in the cup?
A: There isn't any coffee in the cup.

2. Q: How much Coke is there in the bottle?
A: There is some Coke in the bottle.

3. Q: How many tomatoes are there in the fridge?
A: There aren't any tomatoes in the fridge.

4. Q: How much bread is there in the basket?
A: There is some bread in the basket.

5. Q: How much soup is there in the bowl?
A: There isn't any soup in the bowl.

6. Q: How many eggs are there in the fridge?
A: There aren't any eggs in the fridge.

C 1. Every book on this desk is mine.

2. Every worker speaks excellent French.

3. Every waiter starts at 8 a.m.

4. Every animal needs oxygen like human beings.

5. Every boy is playing soccer.

D 1. She drinks three glasses of milk.

2. He eats seven slices/pieces of bread.

3. She drinks five cups of coffee.

4. He can eat four slices/pieces of pizza.

5. She bought three cartons of milk.

Unit 13
Prepositions of Time
p. 78

Learn & Practice 1

A 1. in 2. in 3. On 4. at 5. on 6. In

B 1. on; on 2. at; at 3. at; in 4. on; at 5. in; in 6. in; at 7. on 8. in

Learn & Practice 2

A 1. for 2. during 3. for 4. until 5. before 6. until 7. during 8. during 9. for 10. from 11. before

12. after

Super Writing

A **1.** I have my guitar lessons at 10:00 on Wednesdays

2. School starts at 8 o'clock in the morning.

3. We stayed in Rome for five days.

4. He'll wait for you until 5 o'clock.

5. They go to school at 7 o'clock in the morning.

6. They lived in Korea from 2001 to 2009.

B **1.** No, he didn't. He watched TV for three hours.

2. No, I can't. I can wait for you until 5:30.

3. No, she didn't. She lived in Hong Kong from 2005 to 2011.

4. No, she didn't. She danced until six o'clock in the morning.

C at; in; After/During; At; at; at; in; After; On; at; at; At; On; On; at

E **1.** → He read the newspaper from 7:00 to 7:40.
→ He read the newspaper from 7:00 until 7:40.

2. → He had breakfast from 8:00 to 8:30.
→ He had breakfast from 8:00 until 8:30.

3. → He washed his car from 9:00 to 10:00.
→ He washed his car from 9:00 until 10:00.

4. → He played badminton from 10:00 to 11:00.
→ He played badminton from 10:00 until 11:00.

5. → He went for a walk from 2:00 to 4:00.
→ He went for a walk from 2:00 until 4:00.

Unit 14
Prepositions of Place and Movement p. 84

Learn & Practice 1

A **1.** c **2.** d **3.** a **4.** g **5.** b **6.** e **7.** f

B **1.** in **2.** in **3.** at **4.** on **5.** at **6.** on **7.** on **8.** in
9. in **10.** at

C **1.** above **2.** next to / by **3.** in front of / near
4. between

Learn & Practice 2

A **1.** to **2.** into **3.** across **4.** up **5.** down **6.** through

Super Writing

A **1.** The cat is between the chair and the small table.

2. The schoolbag is under the table.

3. The chair is next to / by the bed.

4. The sneakers are in front of the bed.

5. The books are on the table.

6. The small table is next to / by the bed.

7. The dog is behind the door.

B **1.** They're standing in front of the house.

2. The girl is hiding behind the tree.

3. The dog is between Mia and Emma.

4. They are walking across the street.

C **1.** No, they aren't. They're running down the hill.

2. No, she isn't. She's getting onto the bus.

3. No, it isn't. It is going through the tunnel.

4. No, she isn't. She's getting out of the taxi.

D **1.** Yes, there is. It is opposite the bakery.

2. Yes, there is. It is opposite the music shop. /
It is next to the florist's.

3. Yes, there is. It is between the clothes shop and the fast food restaurant. / It is across from the cinema.

4. Yes, there is. It is next to the bakery. / It is opposite the florist's.

5. Yes, there is. It is next to the cinema. / It is opposite the supermarket. / It is across from the clothes shop.

Unit 15
Helping Verbs 1
p. 90

Learn & Practice 1

A **1.** can **2.** can't **3.** couldn't **4.** couldn't **5.** can't
6. could **7.** can't

Learn & Practice 2

A **1.** should ride **2.** should wear **3.** should eat

B **1.** should **2.** shouldn't **3.** should **4.** should
5. shouldn't

Learn & Practice 3

A **1.** You must not swim here.

2. You must stop.

3. You must not use a cell phone.

4. You must turn left.

B **1.** Do you have to learn Korean?

2. Does Mary have to take an exam?

3. Do the children have to walk home?

Super Writing

A **1.** You must not smoke in the library.

2. You must not run in the hallway.

3. You must not make any noise.

4. You must not eat in the library.

5. You must be careful with the books.

6. You must not leave your phone on the tables when you leave.

7. You must put the books back in the right place.

B **1.** You shouldn't be late for school.

2. You shouldn't come home late.

3. You should do your homework.

4. You should clean your room.

5. You should be nice to your brother and sister.

C **1.** You must fasten your seat belt throughout the flight.

2. You must not smoke in a public place.

3. You don't have to buy a new TV set.

4. You don't have to wear a suit to the office.

5. You don't have to wear safety glasses.

6. You must clean the living room every week.

7. You must not touch statues in the museum.

D **1.** Q: Can you write with your left hand?
A: Yes, I can. / No, I can't.

2. Q: Can you eat with chopsticks?
A: Yes, I can. / No, I can't.

3. Q: Can you ride a snowboard?
A: Yes, I can. / No, I can't.

4. Q: Can you make a kite?
A: Yes, I can. / No, I can't.

5. Q: Can you sing in another language?
A: Yes, I can. / No, I can't.

6. Q: Can you play a musical instrument?
A: Yes, I can. / No, I can't.

Unit 16
p. 96
Helping Verbs 2

Learn & Practice 1

A **1.** Sarah may/might/could be ill.

2. We may/might not go out.

3. It may/might not rain.

4. We may/might/could buy a car.

5. Kevin may/might not be at home.

6. Ann may/might/could need help.

7. Heather may/might not change her job.

Learn & Practice 2

A **1.** May/Could I **2.** Could/Can I **3.** May/Could I

Learn & Practice 3

A **1.** Could you pass me the sugar?

2. Would you give me directions to the city hall?

3. Could you look over this report?

4. Can you wash the dishes for me?

Learn & Practice 4

A **1.** must be **2.** must be **3.** must like **4.** must not like

5. must not be **6.** must not work **7.** must be

Super Writing

A **1.** Would/Could you help me with the exercise?

2. Can you help me with the exercise?

3. Would/Could you fasten your seat belt?

4. Would/Could you open the door?

5. Can you tell me the time?

6. Would/Could you bring me some water?

B **1.** It may rain this afternoon.

2. She might not come to the party.

3. He may not be late.

4. She might pass the exam.

5. They may not be waiting for us.

6. It might not crash.

7. He might have an accident.

C **1.** Can I borrow your dictionary?

2. May/Could I have a glass of water?

3. May/Could I leave early today?

4. May/Could I hand in my homework next week?

5. Can I turn on the TV?

6. May/Could I put my coat here?

D **1.** The restaurant (= It) must not be very good.

2. Ruth (= She) must get very bored with her job.

3. Brian (= He) must like to go to the movies.

4. They must not be home.

5. They must not know many people.

6. Susan (= She) must be sick.

7. Max (= He) must read a lot of books.

Unit 17
p. 102
Infinitives

Learn & Practice 1

A 1. likes to play computer games

2. need to sleep

3. decided to go Singapore

4. would like to have some orange juice

Learn & Practice 2

A

	Verb	Object	Infinitive
1.	told	Karen	to eat
2.	advised	me	to stop
3.	asks	Nancy	to drive
4.	asked	her	to stand up
5.	expect	you	to rewrite
6.	ordered	students	to clean

Learn & Practice 3

A 1. to 2. for 3. for 4. to 5. for 6. to

B 1. to watch the news 2. to learn Korean

3. to see who it was 4. to study economics

5. to buy some books

Super Writing

A 1. her to invite Fred to the party

2. to be/become a famous doctor

3. Sejin to use her smartphone

4. to find a new job

5. Brad to exercise every day

6. the girls to finish their homework

B 1. I went to the post office to mail some letters.

2. I went to a fast food restaurant to eat a hamburger.

3. I went to the bookstore to buy some books.

4. I went to the travel agency to reserve a flight.

5. I went to a movie theater to see a movie.

6. I went to the department store to buy some clothes.

D 1. 1. to take a taxi 2. to lend her some money

3. to brush her teeth after meals

E 1. Jennifer went to Pizza Hut to have dinner.

2. Jennifer went to the library to borrow a book.

3. Jennifer turned up the volume to hear the news better.

4. Jennifer sent an email to Steve to invite him to a party.

5. Jennifer bought a magazine to read an article about her favorite K-pop star.

Learn & Practice 1

A 1. Eating too much (Gerund)

2. Speaking in English (Gerund)

3. The subway (Noun)

4. My dog (Noun)

5. She (Pronoun)

B 1. Learning a foreign language

2. Taking the subway

3. Getting up early in the morning

4. Speaking English well

5. Swimming in the sea

Learn & Practice 2

A 1. mailing 2. preparing 3. to pass 4. asking 5. to go

6. snowing / to snow 7. going / to go

Learn & Practice 3

A 1. goes shopping 2. go swimming 3. go skiing

4. go camping

Super Writing

A 1. Studying math is not easy.

2. Climbing rocks is dangerous.

3. Getting some rest is the most important thing.

4. Learning a language means learning another culture.

5. Saving energy is good for our environment.

B 1. He stopped smoking.

2. She finished eating dinner.

3. They enjoyed listening to music.

4. I avoided answering my phone.

D 1. enjoyed playing the drums; will stop fighting with his brother

2. enjoyed jogging with her father; will stop eating junk food

3. enjoyed riding a bicycle; will stop playing computer games

4. enjoyed eating healthy food; will stop watching soap operas

Unit 19
Need & Want / Would Like
p. 114

Learn & Practice 1
A 1. I need some water.
  2. He wants a new dictionary.
  3. They need to go to school.
  4. He wants to travel around the world.
  5. I need to eat breakfast.

Learn & Practice 2
A 1. A: I'd like a cup of tea.
     N: I wouldn't like a cup of tea.
  2. A: She'd like to go to the theater.
     N: She wouldn't like to go to the theater.
  3. A: They'd like to learn Chinese.
     N: They wouldn't like to learn Chinese.
B 1. Q: Would you like a sandwich? A: I would
  2. Q: Would she like a glass of water?
     A: she wouldn't
  3. Q: Would you like to have a pet? A: I would
  4. Q: Would Tony like to see a movie tonight?
     A: he wouldn't

Learn & Practice 3
A 1. would like to lose 2. likes to swim 3. likes to eat
  4. would like to go 5. would like to go

Super Writing
A 1. would like 2. Would; like to 3. would like to
  4. would like to 5. Would; like 6. would like
B 1. Would you like 2. Do you like 3. Would you like
  4. Do you like 5. Do you like 6. Would you like
  7. Would you like 8. Do you like
C 1. I like to watch the news.
  2. I would like to go to Canada.
  3. I need to go to school at 7:00.
  4. I would like to go to Switzerland.
  5. I like to go fishing with my father.
  6. I wouldn't like to live in an apartment.
D 1. Q: Would you like to become a doctor?
     A: No, I wouldn't. I'd like to become a teacher.
  2. Q: Would Tom like to learn Japanese?
     A: No, he wouldn't. He'd like to learn Korean.
  3. Q: Would you like to have a motorcycle?
     A: No, I wouldn't. I'd like to have a smartphone.

  4. Q: Would Melissa like to go to Japan?
     A: No, she wouldn't. She'd like to go to Egypt.

Unit 20
Comparison
p. 120

Learn & Practice 1
A 1. bigger than 2. faster than 3. taller than
  4. older than

Learn & Practice 2
A 1. prettier 2. busier 3. hotter 4. more slowly
  5. bigger 6. thinner 7. cheaper 8. faster
  9. more expensive 10. older 11. longer
  12. more famous 13. later 14. easier 15. taller
  16. heavier 17. more difficult 18. more quickly
  19. fatter 20. colder 21. happier

Learn & Practice 3
A 1. than 2. as 3. than 4. as 5. as 6. than 7. as 8. as
B 1. My father isn't as old as my mother.
  2. Korea isn't as hot as Thailand.
  3. History isn't as difficult as physics.
  4. The Nile isn't as long as the Amazon.

Super Writing
A 1. Rachel is older than Ava.
  2. Ava is lighter than Rachel.
  3. Rachel is heavier than Ava.
  4. Ava is shorter than Rachel.
  5. Rachel is taller than Ava.
  6. Ava is quieter than Rachel.
  7. Rachel is friendlier than Ava.
B 1. I was as tired as Stacey.
  2. The Han River isn't as clean as the Amazon.
  3. Listening to K-pop music is as interesting as
     watching DMB TV.
  4. A river isn't as big as an ocean.
  5. I didn't study as hard as Rosie.
C 1. as pretty as 2. healthier than 3. as difficult as
  4. as old as 5. as light as 6. more expensive than
D 1. crowded than 2. hotter than 3. rainier than
  4. taller than 5. more modern than 6. faster than